Into That Good Night

Into That Good Night

Ron Rozelle

Farrar • Straus • Giroux

New York

Farrar, Straus and Giroux
19 Union Square West, New York 10003

Copyright © 1998 by Ron Rozelle
All rights reserved
Distributed in Canada by Douglas & McIntyre Ltd.
Printed in the United States of America
Designed by Jonathan D. Lippincott
First edition, 1998

Library of Congress Cataloging-in-Publication Data
Rozelle, Ron, 1952–
    Into that good night / Ron Rozelle.
        p.   cm.
    ISBN 0-374-17711-2
    1. Rozelle, Lester.   2. Alzheimer's disease—Patients—Texas—
Biography.   3. School superintendents—Texas—Biography.
4. Rozelle, Ron, 1952–   .   5. Alzheimer's disease—Patients—
Family relationships.   6. High school teachers—Texas—Biography.
I. Title.
RC523.2.R69   1998
362.1'96831'0092—dc21
[B]   97-43463

Grateful acknowledgment is made to the New Directions Publishing
Corporation for permission to reprint "Into That Good Night" from *The
Collected Poems of Dylan Thomas*, ©1952 by Dylan Thomas. Permission
granted in Canada by J. M. Dent publishers.

For Lester and Quinda
and Diane and Janie

Do not go gentle into that good night,
Old age should burn and rave at close of day;
Rage, rage against the dying of the light.

Though wise men at their end know dark is right,
Because their words had forked no lightning they
Do not go gentle into that good night.

Good men, the last wave by, crying how bright
Their frail deeds might have danced in a green bay,
Rage, rage against the dying of the light.

Wild men who caught and sang the sun in flight,
And then, too late, they grieved it on its way,
Do not go gentle into that good night.

Grave men, near death, who see with blinding sight
Blind eyes could blaze like meteors and be gay,
Rage, rage against the dying of the light.

And you, my father, there on the sad height,
Curse, bless me now with your fierce tears, I pray.
Do not go gentle into that good night.
Rage, rage against the dying of the light.

—Dylan Thomas

Into That Good Night

o n e

It is snowing. Huge, light flakes are drifting and swirling, collecting on the ground and the rooftop and filling up the depression between our yard and Highway 79. This is a rare thing in Oakwood, where it snows once every several years, and then it is, more often than not, a wet, slushy business that melts as it hits, accumulating only in the hollows of trees and in icy bar ditches, leaving finally a dirty mixture best left alone.

It is Christmas Eve eve, as my mother calls the day before Christmas Eve, and it has never, in her memory or mine, snowed this early. Usually, the hard freezes and blue northers come in January or February, dull and useless times spent near heaters or fireplaces, wishing for spring. Mother reports that Warren Culberson, the weatherman on Channel 4 out of Dallas, is sure the snow will stay through Christmas Day. She can quote Mr. Culberson word for word, as she can Paul Crume and Frank X. Tolbert, columnists for the *Dallas Morning News*. The television news and the newspaper are two of my mother's passions (though not on the level of her novels, of which she reads several a week), and she has heroes among their practitioners.

I am nine or ten. Bundled in heavy clothes, I wonder how all this snow, such big flakes of it, can be falling so silently. I am used to winds pounding through the pecan trees and honeysuckle bushes in our yard, or heavy rains trumpeting on our roof and rushing noisily down past my window to splash into puddles. Weather, to my mind, is a loud thing. And now this snow floats so gracefully down to my tongue and my jacket and all the places that I can see and it is quiet. The only sound is from cars and trucks on the highway.

The hedge between our house and Miss Mae's is covered over now, a solid white wall broken only by the gap in its middle that Miss Mae has had Brown cut so that we all can go back and forth more easily. Her house, made of rough, cut stones, sits higher up than ours, on a hill, and the garage end faces us. I walk over to the hedge, listening to the slight crunching beneath my shoes, and see Brown puttering around in the garage. He has been the yardman there for as long as I can remember, and he is my friend. Flossie, the cook, serves him his dinner every day at twelve sharp in a tin plate, and he eats it sitting on an upturned bucket. In the summer, when I'm not in school, I sit on the ground beside him and he gives me his fried hot water corn bread (Flossie cooks it every day). I wonder what Brown will find to keep him busy today, with snow covering everything. We don't have a cook or yardman. Annie Bell comes to help Mother clean our house twice a week, but she never cooks, and her interest in the yard seems limited to the grassless area beneath the fig tree, which she keeps swept clean as a floor.

It is morning, around eight. School is out for the Christmas holidays, and won't start again until after New Year's Day. This gives me ample opportunity to visit with Brown since, on school days, he has already left to sweep at the car dealership in town by the time I get home.

I plod through the gap in the hedge, up the hill, and into the large garage before Brown hears me. He is hard of hearing, and has to lean forward and strain to listen when someone addresses him. Anyone, that is, besides Miss Mae and me; we both talk loud.

Brown is sharpening a knife on a whetstone with his back to me; I kick a clay flowerpot just a little to let him know I'm here. He is a nervous man, and it occurs to me that he might stab himself with the knife if I startle him.

"Moanin," he says, as he slides the kitchen knife along the worn stone.

"Mornin'," I say, plopping myself, in my various coats and sweaters, down on his upturned bucket.

"That snow sho is purty, ain't it?" says Brown. "I ain't never see it snow like dis." He pays close attention to his knife sharpening. "Sho purty. I was jist thinkin' about that comin' from home."

"Did you have to walk in the snow?" I ask him.

"No, suh. Not today. Mr. Robert, he come and get me today in the car. I think Miss Mae, she tell him I can't walk in the snow." He smiles. "I can't, neither. I be slippin' down ever step."

We laugh at this. "Mr. Robert, he say it snow like dis

all the time in the North." Brown speaks of the North as if it is a foreign country, with a border and a gate. "I don't reckon I'd like it all the time." He looks into Miss Mae's backyard, at the shrubs and bushes covered with white. "It sho is purty." He drops a golden bubble of oil on the whetstone and begins sliding another knife along it.

"It don't snow *all* the time in the North," I tell him. "In the summer, it gets hot like here."

Brown looks at me and nods his head, his one good eye wide; his other eye is gone. He sometimes wears a glass eye in the socket, not today. He seems to enjoy everything I tell him.

"What'll you do today?" I ask him.

"Gots to finish these here knifes for Flossie fust thing," he says. "She like a sharp edge on her kitchen knives." He inspects a knife with his one eye, as if he just reminded himself of this. "Then I'll probly bresh the snow offen the bushes." He gives this some thought. I think he figures that snow can't be doing them any good.

I don't know anything about it. But I offer an opinion anyway; Brown will think I know. "Snow won't hurt those bushes. There's water in snow." This is news to him; I can tell. He squints his eye and considers it before grinning. All new information is received by Brown with a grin. "Besides," I say, "it's still snowing. Warren Culberson says it'll snow all morning, and then it'll stick till after Christmas."

Brown ponders this. I don't know whether he is in awe of the fact that it will snow all morning, or if he's wondering who Warren Culberson is, or if he is deciding what to do instead of removing the snow from the bushes.

He looks, again, at the blanket of white that is covering everything. "It sho is purty," he says. His breath becomes a cloud of vapor in the cold air.

I hear our back door open down the hill, and my mother calls me.

"I'll be back later, Brown," I say. "Don't knock the snow off those bushes." I get up off the bucket and walk into the falling snow. Brown comes out into it also. His skin is even blacker and shinier than usual against all this white. "Miss Mae probably wants 'em nice and pretty."

"Yes, suh," he quickly agrees. "I 'spect she does."

Walking back through the gap in the hedge, I am careful not to knock any snow off. Any advice I give to Brown should, I think, be followed by me. He is, after all, the only person I can give advice to.

Once inside the warmth of our utility room, I gradually emerge from the sweaters and coat, leaving them piled on the tile along with my shoes. By my mother's decree, we always leave our shoes by the door. My sister, Janie, at a stage in life where not much that goes on around here sits too well with her, says we might as well be a bunch of Japanese.

My breakfast is almost ready. Mother is at the stove in one of her orange housedresses, cooking French toast. I spend a good bit of my time watching her cook. When I was little, before I went to school, I shadowed her all day long, not missing much that she did.

Mother subscribes to three book clubs, one of which is the Cookbook Guild. She receives a new cookbook every month and, whatever its subject or length, reads it from cover to cover. From the recipes in these books, she prepares rich, exotic dishes which are pretty much lost on the common tastes of the rest of us.

As the toast, soaked in its egg batter, sizzles in the skillet, I watch my mother take long pulls from her Pall Mall cigarette, one of about forty that she will smoke today. When the color of the bread is to her liking, she lifts it to a plate and sprinkles it with sugar. This she brings to the table with a mug of hot chocolate.

"Why does Brown say 'yes, sir' and 'no, sir' to me?" I ask through a mouthful of French toast.

She is wiping her stove clean with a dishrag. "It's just his way," she says. "Brown is very respectful and nice." She takes a sip from a mug of black coffee which is never more than an arm's length away during the morning hours. "He's one of the most respectful people in creation." She picks a tiny speck of tobacco from her lip. "Mostly it's respect for your daddy. Brown has children in the Dunbar school, and your daddy's their superintendent too."

"Does Brown say 'sir' to Negro children?"

"No," Mother says, "I don't imagine he does." She is now washing her heavy iron skillet in the sink. "And he shouldn't say it to you either. You can't go around expecting grown people to 'yes, sir' and 'no, sir' you." She is looking out the window over the sink; maybe she's looking at Brown up in Miss Mae's garage. "And," she says, turning to point her Pall Mall at me, "I don't want you eating his corn bread anymore. Janie says you eat it every day in the summer." Her kitchen is clean now, and she surveys it. "Brown works hard and *needs* his lunch. Don't you eat it anymore."

"But he gives it to me," I tell her.

"I didn't say anything about Brown offering," she says, grinding her cigarette into an orange ashtray; "I'm talking about you taking it." Once again she peeks out the window at the snow. "Put your plate in the sink when you're finished, and come look at the tree with me."

Our Christmas tree is a cedar which Mr. Headley Eldridge cut for us on his land. We are town people, with no access to trees for cutting, and Mr. Headley, a housepainter and one of my father's closest friends, brought us this one. It is taller than me and even taller than Mother.

In the living room, she plugs in the lights and we step back to look at it. We share a deep appreciation for the magic of Christmas and all things Christmasy; we spend much of our time looking at this tree, and hours huddled over the Sears, Roebuck catalog all through the fall before Mother finally scribbles, in her hen scratch, the big order. More hours are spent wrapping every present just so on top of the deep freezer in the utility room. And sometimes we drive to town, a little more than a mile up the highway, just to look at the plywood Nativity scene at the Methodist church.

She pulls open the venetian blinds behind the tree to give it a backdrop of snow. "I've never in my life seen a Christmas tree in front of falling snow," she says, as she pulls me close to her.

"Me neither," I say.

"Well, of course you haven't." She laughs, hugging me tighter. "If I haven't, you haven't."

"I hope it snows all through Christmas," I say, too loud.

"Shh," Mother hisses, "you'll wake up Janie." She continues to look at the huge snowflakes drifting down slowly behind our tree. "It won't keep snowing that long. But the snow on the ground will stay there and be pretty for Christmas Day."

"In two more days," I say, pressing the side of my face against her. I can smell her bath powder.

"In two more days," she says.

It is late at night now. I am snuggled deep into my bed, watching the brightest of the winter stars through my window. I have raised the window just a bit to let in some of the cold air near my head. The house is too warm for me and, besides, I want the crisp air to remind me of how cold it is outside, and of the snow, and Christmas. Everyone else is asleep; I can hear my father's rhythmic snoring down the hall. I like the idea, as I burrow deeper into the sheets and pull the blanket and quilt over me, that the whole town must be sleeping now, everybody warm and safe and in their proper places.

My mother and father are in the twin double beds in their long bedroom at the rear of the house. They both snore like sawmills, but I can only hear my father at the moment. At the opposite end of the house, in the front bedroom, is Janie, in high school now and beyond us all. I am a particular problem for her; my very existence seems to be a constant blight on her world. She snaps at me a lot, and sometimes even at Mother, but never with the steam that she aims in my direction. The only person who is immune from her current disposition is my father; Janie and my father pretty much think the other one hung the moon. Diane, my oldest sister, so many years my senior that she was grown and married before I knew her at all, is, no doubt, entwined with her husband, Jimmy—it's been my observation that they sleep awfully close to-gether—across town in their tiny rent house filled with clothes and furniture and pots and pans handed down from our home to theirs. In the room adjoining Jimmy and Diane's are Lisa and Greg, piled into a sofa bed, and, in her bassinet, Lynn. I was only five when Lisa was born, and Mother had considerable difficulty convincing me that I was her uncle and not her grandfather.

Sitting up to look out the window, I search for Bo, the latest in a long line of our dogs which fell victim to the highway, and the only survivor. A car or truck ran over Bo's forelegs, shattering both badly. My father, who ei-ther is ignorant of the existence of veterinary medicine or shuns it as extravagant, gently attached makeshift splints to Bo's legs in the garage. Bo let him do it, and his eyes told us that he knew that my father was trying to help

him. Since the splints were removed, Bo has had to crawl along with his forelegs out in front and his behind in the air, propelled entirely by his rear legs. His most comfortable position is to sit squarely on his rear, with his forelegs hanging loosely and his head in the air, as if begging. The sight of a large black dog sitting upright in our yard has impressed more than one passerby, and Bo has become something of a conversation piece hereabouts. Looking for him now—and he should be easy enough to find, perched ramrod straight—I see only our snow-covered yard washed in moonlight. I imagine Bo is sound asleep in the well house behind the fig tree, burrowed into a warm corner, his sad face resting on his misshapen legs.

Miss Mae and Mr. Robert are up the hill, warm and snoozing within the rough-cut stones of the big house. Down the hall from them is Mr. Mack, Mr. Robert's brother and his partner in the Chevrolet dealership in town. The name of the dealership is Greer Brothers, and that is where Brown sweeps every afternoon, after working in Miss Mae's yard all day. Since Mr. Mack never married, the Greer Brothers work with each other every day, and go home to the same house every night. Mr. Mack, old and nearly toothless, is now, I imagine, snoring into the pillows of the big bed in his bedroom at the back of the house.

Elsewhere, Annie Bell and Brown are sleeping in other houses. Whenever Mother and I go to collect Annie Bell, or drop her off, I stare at the small, dilapidated structure that is her home. It seems to me that a good gust of north

wind would bring it down completely. But Annie Bell couldn't be prouder of it if it were a palace. She keeps her yard swept clean, as she does the area beneath our fig tree; not one blade of grass is in evidence.

I've never seen Brown's house, but I think it must be much the same. Annie Bell and Brown and their families are sleeping now, and waiting for Christmas like the rest of us. When I think about the plywood Nativity scene in front of the Methodist church in town, I imagine the original manger, all of those hundreds of years ago, must have looked more like Annie Bell's and Brown's houses than like Miss Mae's, or even ours.

From far off, I hear the slow rumble of a train, coming from the north. This will be the Eagle, on its run from St. Louis to as far south as San Antonio. I listen as it approaches, and then I look out my window to watch it pass beyond the pasture across the highway. Most of the lights in the train are out, so even the people in there must be sleeping; only one car seems to house activity. Trains don't stop at our little depot anymore, but fly through town at full speed, whistle screaming and bells clanging. Once, when the train still made a stop here, we all rode it to Austin, then got on another train and came right back. I think that my father, who had ridden trains for years, didn't want his children to grow up without having ridden one. It was high adventure, and we all enjoyed it, even Janie, who wasn't in high school yet, and could still enjoy such things.

Oakwood is quiet now that the train has passed. When

I lie back on my pillow and close my eyes, I can see every store in town, as if I were walking down the sidewalks in the cold moonlight. In my mind, I see the hulking two-story clapboard hotel, a pathetic relic of another era, a long-ago time full of cotton and prosperity. Pieces of it fall away with each passing year, moving it further and further beyond the help of paint and fixing. Beside the hotel is the post office, where my father goes every morning to collect the school's mail and ours. Mr. Son Coates, one of my father's friends, works here. Mr. Buck Moore, a rural mail carrier and my father's best friend, sorts his letters and parcels here each early morning before driving into the country to deliver them. Next, behind my closed eyes, I see Dixon's drugstore. As a young teacher and coach who had only recently moved here from Alto, my father once borrowed enough money from Mr. Dixon to travel with him by train to Chicago to see the World's Fair and, much more important to my father, to see a professional baseball game. It took him two years to pay the money back, each month, on schedule.

Next is our bank, so absolutely in the center of town, at the intersection of the two major streets, that its location is known to everyone as the "bank corner," a landmark as meaningful to us as those ancient town crosses are to English villages. Our mayor, Mr. Roddy Rawls Wiley, is the president of the bank, as his father was before him. It is Mr. Roddy Rawls who, on election nights, is in constant telephone communication with the courthouse in Centerville, the county seat, and it is he who paints, in a thick paste made of Bon Ami cleanser and water, the county results of various races on the windows of the bank. These numbers, tallied by precinct, tell the assembled town people and country folk, sitting on their cars and in the backs of pickup trucks, who will be the next road commissioner and sheriff and judge. It was to these windows that such a congregation looked to find, just a couple of years ago, that a young Catholic (of all things) from Massachusetts would succeed President Eisenhower. Tonight, I imagine the bank is cold and dark, its artificial Christmas tree barely visible through the tall windows which seem to be perpetually clean from the yearly applications of Bon Ami.

Around the corner is Mr. Duncan Dorman's barbershop, a musty room which smells always of dust and talcum and tobacco where my father and I go to get our crew cuts. Here is Miss Tine Lambert's five-and-ten-cent store, where she and Miss Reba Faye sell various and sundry items from an inventory which, more than likely, predates the Second World War, and maybe the First. It is to this cluttered shop that my father will come late tomorrow afternoon, on Christmas Eve, to make his holiday purchases. They are always inexpensive and simple offerings, bought at the last minute in a place with little to offer. But they are his special gifts to all of us, not to be compared to or confused with the more elaborate ones that Mother has long since wrapped and placed under the tree.

Here is Miss Pearl Hardin's grocery, Joe Earl Moore's

television shop (he only sells and repairs Zeniths, so we all watch Zeniths), and Marie's, one of two beauty shops for white ladies, the other being located in Miss Selma Shaw's front room.

Laurene's Cafe is around the corner, where we go for our Sunday dinner after church—roast beef or fried steak with mashed potatoes and English peas, with a dollop of fruit salad in the exact center—and where I try to watch, through the door which opens into the kitchen, the black people being served at a counter behind the stoves and accessible by a side entrance.

In the next block, the only other one, is the feed store, and behind it, the Melba Theater, a movie house which closed down last year, and will be renovated into a wash-ateria. New signs have already been painted over the doors: "White" and "Colored."

Mr. Deck Moore's drugstore is just up the street, and Johnson's grocery and, at the corner, Bobby Stroud's hardware store. Bobby's sons, Jim Bob and Tim, are friends of mine and I always volunteer to go with my father, when he announces that he is going to the hardware, in hopes of seeing one or both of them. While my father settles into one of the chairs around the heater, joining several other men who make it their daily business to make up Bobby's court, Jim Bob and Tim and I rummage through the dusty bins and shelves. Anything dropped, like washers or bolts or nails, stands about a fifty-fifty chance of rolling through one of the numerous cracks in the wooden floor to be lost forever, or at least until that day when the cavernous building is finally pulled down and a treasure trove of hardware is discovered on the ground.

Behind my squinched eyes I see the old, high-ceilinged store in cold darkness tonight. The majestic stuffed deer, one of Bobby's victims of some season past, stands sentinel over row upon row of dusty wares. The deer's glass eyes reflect only the moonlight which comes in the high, dirt-caked windows. Nobody leaves their lights on at night, except in some of the houses as a comfort against the darkness. We don't worry too much about evildoers; most people don't even lock their doors. I can smell the hardware store, musty and leathery and metallic, like a nickel held tight in a sweaty palm on a hot day.

Flossie's dress shop and the Bus Stop Cafe make up the rest of the block. Mr. Robert and Mr. Mack's business, Greer Brothers Chevrolet, is across the highway, as is the small city hall. There are three gas stations and, across the tracks, beyond the depot, Mr. Jack Lipsey's engine repair shop and several stores which cater to blacks. The white school, grades one through twelve, separated in the middle of the long, red-bricked building by my father's office, is up the hill by the cemetery. Dunbar, the black school, is across town. My father is the superintendent of both schools, but he leaves the administration of Dunbar to Mr. J. G. Oliver, its principal, known to the town, both black and white, as Professor Oliver. He is well educated, and maintains a vocabulary superior to that of probably everyone in Oakwood. Once, when he telephoned our house and asked to speak to my father, Janie told him that she would go and get him. "Oh, no, young lady," Professor Oliver said, "I don't wish to discommode him." To which my sister replied, "Don't worry, he's not on the commode."

It's a small town, though in its heyday it was the largest in Leon County. The population sign on the highway has never deviated from 716 in my lifetime. There is no hospital, or even a single doctor or dentist. No newspaper, no lawyer, no funeral home. For those, we depend on Palestine, almost twenty miles away, and, now that the Melba is closed, for movies as well. Our tall television antennas, which shoot up from most of the houses like unmowed weeds, pick up the three Dallas stations and one from Tyler. Every now and then, we can get one or two of the Houston stations, but nobody tries very hard since most people figure that if they can't find something to watch on four channels, they are just too hard to please. There is an abundance of churches around town and in the countryside. A few Catholics drive into Palestine for services; we have no Jews to my knowledge, and there are several fundamentalist congregations. Mostly, we are Baptists and Methodists. My family is Methodist.

The people here are, for the most part, not educated beyond the local school. They do a day's work every day and raise families and feed them. What little savings they can scrape together goes into Mr. Roddy Rawls's bank, but usually doesn't stay there long. Most folks have a garden and many have cows and chickens. Oakwood's people live their lives out in much the same way, and along the same schedule, as generations of their ancestors have before them, following the ancient pull of the seasons, and simply doing the best that they can. It's not uncommon for someone to die in the same room they were born in, perhaps in the same bed. I'm thinking of them all now, the whole town, asleep in their beds and dreaming their many dreams.

A big truck is coming fast down the highway from the south, from Buffalo. I have become quite an expert at telling if trucks are full or empty by spending hours at night listening as they pass our house. This one is empty; it rattles and groans as it descends the hill, its great, hollow insides shifting and swaying. As it reaches the bottom of the hill near our house the driver begins to slow down as he sees the town up ahead. He sees, I know, the colored Christmas lights stretched out over Highway 79. He might notice the Nativity scene beside the Methodist church. He is probably from far away, this driver. From San Antonio, or Missouri, or Chicago. In daylight, he might have stopped for a hamburger or a piece of pie at the Bus Stop Cafe or at Laurene's. But now, in the middle of the night, our town is nothing more to him than a place to slow down for. He won't have even glimpsed the story of the town, or its meaning. He will see, if he is sufficiently awake or interested, a few of the houses and the stores, and will know nothing of the lives that are played out, daily, in them. There seems something not right about his piercing through, in a matter of seconds, my entire world.

In a few hours, our house and the town will wake up

and it will be Christmas Eve. Daylight will come, and coffee and breakfasts will be put on tables in warm kitchens with frost on their windows. Lights will flicker on in the houses, and the stores will begin, one by one, to come to life, beginning with Johnson's grocery, where Mr. Lancaster Johnson will sit and smoke and watch the cold morning brighten through his window and wait for Oakwood to wake up. The Butternut Bakery truck will leave loaves of bread, still warm in their wrappers, in the breadboxes at the grocery stores and cafes. Fires will be lit. Husbands and wives and children will be hugged and patted, and, in some cases, simply smiled at or nodded to. Lives will go on.

I don't hear the truck now, or any other sounds. I focus on my bright star and feel the cold seeping in beneath my window and know that sleep, like the heavy stillness and quiet of the town after the train rolled through, will come soon.

It's as though I'm the only person awake in the world.

My father is moving firewood from the large pile beside the garage to a smaller stack he maintains on the front porch. He is pushing the wood in an old wheelbarrow which is too heavy for me to push without tipping it over. Each wheelbarrow load holds a precise amount, for my father has determined exactly how many trips with how many sticks will be needed to make the stack complete. He goes about this as carefully as he calculates the best way to solve an algebra problem or center a page heading in the math and typing classes he teaches at the high school.

He buys wood each year from a farmer who, having delivered and stacked it neatly into a cord, steps back while my father, with a yardstick, measures the length and height of the pile to be sure that both he and the farmer have been well served in the transaction.

It is early morning on Christmas Eve. My father worked in his office at the school all day yesterday and will be home today and tomorrow. I help him load the wood into the wheelbarrow and unload it on the porch. He tells me to lay the sticks neatly in the wheelbarrow so they will ride well. I walk along beside him as he pushes the wood, and I can sense the strain that he feels moving the heavy load through the snow. He is bareheaded, and his scalp, red from the cold, shines through his short, white crew cut. His hands and arms are strong and, like his legs, stocky and sinewy; he played and coached football as a young man. But he is well over fifty now, much older than any of my friends' fathers, and much too old, to my thinking, to be pushing heavy loads.

It stopped snowing yesterday, just as Mother and Warren Culberson had predicted, but the ground is still covered, although considerably tracked up with footprints, mostly mine. Late yesterday afternoon Mother and I put on our warmest clothes and searched until we located, behind the holly bush in the furthermost corner of our yard, what we considered to be the cleanest, purest snow on the place. This my mother carefully removed with a large serving spoon, placing it into a mixing bowl and carrying it into the kitchen, where she stirred it, with sugar and vanilla and milk, into snow ice cream. We sat on the floor in the living room and ate while we studied all the ornaments on the tree, reevaluating where we had placed them, and discussing their histories and meanings. When Mother finished her ice cream, she pulled her thin legs up under her chin and smoked a Pall Mall.

Once we have replenished our stack on the porch, my father and I carry several sticks of wood inside so that he can build the first fire of the day. I like to watch him lay a fire, a procedure to which he pays such close attention that he might as well be doing brain surgery. First, he and I choose, from among several unsplit sections of wood on the porch, what we judge to be a good backlog. In the living room, he uses a scoop and brush to remove all the ashes from yesterday's fires; these he puts into a bucket kept in the garage for just this purpose. Next, he pushes the winner of our backlog competition onto the back of the grate and bundles strips of yesterday's newspaper in front of it. Over this, he lightly places small lengths of pine kindling before finally arranging, with great care, two or three sections of oak and pecan. After studying his work, and making sure that the structure is loose enough for the chimney to draw sufficient air through it to make our fire catch and blaze, he lets me strike the single match and touch it to the corner of the bundled paper that sets it all into motion. When it is roaring, and the pine kindling is oozing its rich sap, hissing and steaming, into the inferno, he goes into the kitchen to begin our breakfast, a chore he takes over from Mother on weekends and holidays.

This gives me the opportunity to sort and shake and rearrange the gifts under the tree, an enterprise which I've undertaken much too often in my mother's opinion. Some of the presents are breakable, she always tells me, and, after being jostled about all the time, will, no doubt, on Christmas morning, fall out in pieces all over creation when unwrapped. Janie has warned me not to so much as touch any of her presents. Mother is, however, at this moment occupied somewhere in the back of the house, and Janie is fast asleep in her bedroom.

Lisa, Greg, and Lynn (Diane's kids) and Janie and I seem to have made the best haul this year. These gifts I have already isolated and stacked in separate piles. I decide now, though, that the suspense will be greater in the morning if I rearrange them randomly, so that their distribution will take longer. I am in the middle of doing just that when I hear Mother in the kitchen, telling my father to remember to load film into the school's portable movie camera so he can record all the doings in the morning. I judge that the gift reorganization will be best left for another time.

I settle myself in my usual place at the kitchen table and wait for my pancakes; my father always cooks pancakes with sausage or bacon. Tomorrow, as a treat for Christmas, he will fry a special mixture of venison and pork which his cousin Hubert Willis, the owner of Tip Top Meats in Tyler, sends to us each year. Today, he's turning strips of bacon over in the sizzling grease in the iron skillet.

"Diane and the kids will be over this afternoon," my mother says as she gets plates down from the cabinet.

"What about Jimmy?" my father asks. Jimmy Smart is Diane's husband. He had been one of the best six-man football players in Texas when he was in Oakwood High School. He could have, according to my father, gone to any college he wanted to on a football scholarship. Now, several years later, he is married and the father of three small children, living in a small rented house and working long, hard days away from home on pipelines for Mr. Tight Lipsey.

"He's on a job," Mother says, placing knives and forks and syrup and butter on the table. "He won't be in till after midnight." She takes a long pull from her coffee, and another from her Pall Mall.

"That's too bad," my father says. He is lifting the last of the bacon onto paper towels, where he pats it dry of grease. Next he cracks four eggs into the popping grease in the skillet, two for him and one each for Mother and me, and begins sloshing the grease in waves over the eggs with a spatula. Janie will eat something later, a pancake maybe; she wouldn't touch an egg with a stick, much less eat one.

"He'll make it for the presents in the morning," Mother says. "Diane said she and the kids will sleep here

24

tonight, since Jimmy won't be home till late." She looks out the window over the sink. "I hope the roads won't be frozen over."

"They will be," my father says, not taking his eyes from the crisp edges of the eggs. "But there won't be any snow or ice on them." He lifts the eggs to the plates. "He'll be all right."

I am thinking about the pancakes my father will now cook on the griddle that has been heating up on two of the burners. The runny yolk of my egg will soak into my pancakes and it will all feel like a sponge when I eat it.

"Why won't there be any snow on the roads?" I ask.

He is pouring the grease from the skillet into a coffee can; he tilts a little out on the griddle. "All the cars that drive on the roads melt it off," he says.

I file this bit of information away so that I can share it with Brown later.

After we finish our breakfast, and my mother and father are busy cleaning up the kitchen, making it ready for all the cooking Mother will do today for Christmas, I bundle up and go out to check on Bo. I have to break the ice in his water bowl and go into the kitchen to refill it. All of the outside faucets are wrapped with towels and rope to keep them from freezing.

Bo is confused by the snow, I think. Or maybe it is particularly cold for him since he has to scoot along on his belly. He has stayed, the last couple of days, pretty close to the well house. He whimpers and looks at me with his sad eyes as he noisily laps up the water and I stroke his back. He is, on the whole, a sad dog. And his constant whine and look of despair do nothing to cheer any of us up. But he's been through a lot, and we love him. I can't remember if he was this sad before his accident, or if it was brought on by that particular trauma.

Leaving Bo to the warm corner of the well house, where my father has put down an old blanket for him, I head up, through the gap in the hedge, to Miss Mae's. I don't see Brown anywhere in the garage or the yard. It crosses my mind that, if he had to walk to work today, he might have, as he predicted, slipped and fallen in the snow.

Flossie opens the door when I knock and says good morning. As I walk through the kitchen, I see that she is already hard at work on holiday cooking. I can see a huge turkey through the window of the top oven; a good smell—mincemeat, maybe—comes from the lower one.

Miss Mae sits in her robe in one of the overstuffed chairs by the fire in her den, reading glasses perched on the tip of her nose, the crossword from the morning paper in her lap, pencil in her teeth, and a cup of coffee in its saucer on the side table.

"Ronnnie," she yells (she talks as loud as I do). Every time she sees me, which is usually several times a day, she seems excited, as if we hadn't laid eyes on each other for months. Dropping the pencil, she removes her glasses and taps them on the arm of the empty chair beside hers. "Come sit with me!" Miss Mae's reading glasses are in constant motion. She puts them on and takes them off again many hundreds of times each day. She points with them, taps them to make a point, and, when thinking, holds them to her lips or her temple.

"Are you workin' the puzzle?" I ask as I sit down.

"Oh, honey," she shouts. "I'm trying." On go the glasses. "That's about all."

"Where is Brown?" I ask her.

"Humph," she grunts, obviously disgusted. "Robert just called from the garage that he has Brown down there with two of his *children*!" She so emphasizes the last word, with a hard tap of her glasses (which are off again), that I am uncertain as to whether she is upset that Brown has two children on the premises of Greer Brothers, or that he has been so irresponsible as to father children at all.

"Why are they down there?" I ask.

She sighs, and puts on her glasses, as if they might let her more clearly see the misery of this current dilemma, so that she might better relay it to me.

"Robert went to get Brown this morning," she begins, "because of the snow. Well, when he got there he found out that Brown's wife has up and gone to Palestine with somebody and left Brown with these children. So Robert loaded the whole mess up and took them to town. Then he called me to see if I wanted them on the place all day." She drinks some of her coffee with such relish that I imagine that she is fueling up for the next onslaught. "I need Brown to bring me some firewood, then they can all go back to town and Robert can find something for him to do down there."

Mr. Robert himself walks in, an ever-present cigar lodged securely in the corner of his mouth. His brother, Mr. Mack, always wears a cigar, too, but Mr. Robert actually smokes his occasionally.

"Hi, Runnie," he says, without looking at me or removing the cigar, and, to Miss Mae, "Brown's fixing to move the wood down from the hill."

"What I want to know is," yells Miss Mae, "why one of Brown's girls can't look after those children." She squints her eyes and points the glasses at Mr. Robert. "He has a houseful old enough to do that."

"Well, I don't know," he says. "All I know is that when I got there he had those boys with him." He picks up a section of the newspaper and studies it. "He didn't want to leave them by themselves."

"Well, they needn't think they'll have the run of this place," Miss Mae yells as I head for the back door to look at these children. "I'll tell you that."

"I don't know anything about it," Mr. Robert says as he settles into the chair I've just vacated. He begins to read the paper.

Outside, I see that Brown has made his way up the hill with a wheelbarrow, his two sons following behind him.

Miss Mae's house sits on a level section of a hill with another hill behind it. There is a big backyard full of shade trees, row after row of plants and shrubs, and, at one end, surrounded by a curving box hedge, a fishpond lined with the same rough-cut stones the house is built of. The woodpile is situated far back on the topmost hill, and Brown and his boys are almost to it.

I run up the hill to catch them and, when I get there, I stop and stare at the two boys. I've never seen any of Brown's children before and am surprised that, though his features are on them, they don't look too much like him. They are watching Brown move the wheelbarrow close to the stack. I think they must be awfully cold in the light, ragged jackets and second- or third-hand shoes they are wearing.

"Mornin', Brown," I say.

He catches me in his good eye. "Moanin," he says. "I had to bring my boys wid me this moanin." He nods in their direction, as if to help me ascertain that these are the boys he is speaking of.

The boys, one about my age and the other a couple of years younger, look at me. The younger one's eyes seem as wide as saucers, and he has a wide, toothy grin.

"I'm gonna tote some of this here wood down to the house," Brown announces; I don't know if it is to me or to his sons. "I sho hope they ain't no snakes in it."

"Snakes are asleep now," I tell him. "They sleep all through the winter." I'm pretty sure this is true, but I'm glad Brown will be poking around in the big stack and not me.

All four of us look at the wood in silence, as if not to wake the snakes.

The older of Brown's boys moves closer to his father and whispers something to him. Brown, of course, can't hear a word of it. "Talk up!" he shouts.

The boy looks embarrassed and, seeing no way around it, speaks loudly enough for us all to hear. "Kin we go look at them flowerpots over yonder?" He nods toward a stack of clay pots at the very back of Miss Mae's property.

Brown looks at the stack of pots, at his sons, at me, then back at the pots. "I reckon so," he finally says. "Don't you go nowhere down around that house." He turns away and begins to carefully dislodge a stick of wood, training his one eye on anything that might be lurking in the stack.

The boys move off in the direction of the pots and I, curious to see what the big attraction is, follow them. When I get there, the older boy is brushing off one of the larger pots and lifting it to get a better look.

"Miss Mae plants flowers in those," I tell him. He says nothing, but continues his examination. "Some of them are broken," I say, as I walk to where several of the pots lay in fragments. The younger boy, his eyes still wide, follows me. His brother doesn't seem interested.

"You go to Dunbar?" I ask the younger boy.

He nods that he does.

"What grade?" I ask him.

He says nothing, but stares at the broken pots.

"My daddy is the superintendent of Dunbar," I tell him.

The older boy, still holding the pot he is so interested in, says, without looking up, "Puhfessur Oliver is the head of it."

The younger boy nods that this is so.

"But my daddy is the superintendent," I maintain. "He's Professor Oliver's boss."

An expression comes over both boys' faces which says that it is not even remotely possible that Professor Oliver would have a boss.

"I ain't never seen yo daddy at Dunbar," says the older boy.

I consider this, and, at the moment, can't think of a reason for it.

The older boy has completed his inspection and is wiping snow from his hands. After a period of time in which neither of us speaks (I've given up on the younger boy saying anything), I start walking, past Miss Mae's pear trees, toward home. The bare and twisted limbs of the trees stretch out against the slate-gray sky like skeletons reaching out for something.

"He in the fust grade," the older boy calls to me. I turn to look at him. "I in the foth," he continues. The younger boy's grin becomes, if possible, even wider.

"Why'd you want to look at those pots?" I ask the older one.

He studies them, then shrugs as if to say it doesn't matter.

The younger boy is scraping some snow along with his shoe. "You ever build a snowman?" I ask him. He shakes his head that he has not, and, after a good bit of encouragement on my part, we begin one. After a while, the older boy starts to help, and, by the time Brown comes up the hill to tell the boys it is time to leave, we have assembled a small creature which, if much imagination is employed, might be thought to be in the shape of a human. I look around until I find three small shards of broken pottery to serve as eyes and a nose, then the older boy and I manipulate two sticks into position for arms. He is a pitiful thing, our snowman, and he looks at home among the smashed pots.

I go home to ask permission to ride to town with Mr. Robert to deliver Brown and his sons to Greer Brothers, where Brown will sweep and clean. My father is sitting by the fire, reading the *Dallas Morning News*. I find Mother in the kitchen, rolling the dough that will be the crusts for her pecan and sweet potato pies. I tell her about Brown's boys and ask to go to town with Mr. Robert. Janie is up now and is at the table with a half-eaten pancake on the plate in front of her. Her feet are crossed in the chair beside her and she is gazing into a well-worn hardback copy of *Gone with the Wind*, which she and some of her friends have read several times. They seem to be trying to outdo each other in this odd competition. Her copy came from the bookstore my mother had run in the front room of her parents' big house in Livingston during the Second World War. After the war, she married my father and he brought her, along with her seven-year-old daughter and the entire inventory of the bookshop, to Oakwood, where he resumed his position as Superintendent of Schools after his Army service in the South Pacific.

As I go out the front door, I turn and ask my father why he never visits the Dunbar school.

"Mr. Oliver runs Dunbar," he says, still intent on his newspaper. "I just go over there to see him." He turns the page. "And to give awards sometimes." Brown's boys, I figure, as I run back up the hill, must not win awards.

I sit in the front seat with Mr. Robert on the way to town; Brown and his sons ride in the back seat. Nobody says anything.

When we get there, Mr. Robert tells me that we will be going home soon and he goes into his office. I say good morning to Mr. Mack, who is in his usual place, a metal lawn chair in the corner of the showroom by the window, where he can see everything that goes on outside. A large unlit cigar is clamped in his toothless gums; his trousers are pulled up to the middle of his chest.

Brown and his boys have gone back into the big garage area and Brown is already scattering handfuls of red sawdust on the concrete floor to absorb the grease and oil before he sweeps. The two boys are standing near a wall, watching one of the mechanics work on an engine and being careful to stay out of the way. The mechanic doesn't pay them any attention, but, when I join them, he looks at the three of us for a moment before going back to his work.

"Come on," I say to the older boy, "let's go outside."

On the ground, beside some oil drums at the side of the building, we find several washers and, clearing a small area at the base of the wall, begin to play a game that is obviously common to Oakwood children of all races. The older boy is better at it than I am, and he usually wins. The younger boy doesn't participate, nor is he invited to. His broad grin seems to say he's happy watching.

The older boy and I limit our conversation to groans and murmurs which indicate our success or failure in tossing the washers as close to the wall as possible.

"I whist I had one of them pots," he says suddenly.

I have to think a moment to remember that he is talking about the pile of pots on Miss Mae's hill.

"What for?" I ask him.

He picks up the washers from the ground. "I whist I had one for my mama to put flowers in," he says, looking at the washers.

It's hard for me to imagine Brown, who spends so much of his time tending to flowerpots, not having any at his own house.

"Maybe Miss Mae will give you one," I say, tossing a washer not very close to the wall.

His expression tells me that he considers this unlikely.

We return to our game and are so absorbed in it that three boys are behind us before we hear them. These are three brothers who go to school with me who live somewhere out near the Ninevah community. Two of the brothers are in my grade because the oldest one was kept back one year. The other brother is in the grade just below ours and, since, in our school, two grades are combined in one room with one teacher, he shares a classroom with us every other year.

The younger of Brown's boys, his grin still in place, backs up when he sees the three brothers.

"What you doin', Ronnie?" one of the three brothers asks.

I put my hands in the pockets of my jacket and look at the ground. "Pitchin' washers," I say. I can hear a train coming toward town from the south.

The three brothers look at Brown's boys, who look at me. I look at the ground.

"These some of your friends?" the oldest of the three brothers, grinning, asks me, pointing to Brown's boys.

One of the brothers nudges him and all three begin to laugh. After a moment, I laugh with them.

"They're Brown's boys," I say. Not knowing what else to say, I ask them what they are doing in town.

"My daddy's tractor is broke," one of the boys says. He unwraps two small pieces of hard candy (root beer logs, I think) and pushes them into the back of his jaw, like tobacco. "He come to get a part for it." He spits some of the candy juice on the ground, making a perfect brown circle in the dirty snow.

Mr. Robert calls me from his car.

"I have to go," I tell the three brothers from Ninevah, and start walking toward Mr. Robert's car.

"Ain't you taking your friends home with you?" one of the three brothers calls after me. I can barely hear them laughing over the growing rumble of the train.

I turn to face the three brothers and, after stealing a glance at Brown's boys, stand still and listen to the freight train roll through town. The crossing signal is clanging and I am thinking of my classroom at school, where I will return next week. The three brothers will be there, too. Brown's boys will not be there.

"They ain't my friends," I yell over the noise of the train and the clanging.

The three brothers laugh and Brown's older boy turns to go into the garage. Before he does, though, I see, in the downturned corner of his lip and in the narrowness of his eyes that he knows that it had to come to this, that these are the rules, old and hard, and nothing so simple as a game of washers or the construction of a snowman will make even a dent in them. He seems almost relieved to have some inner knowledge proven right.

Mr. Robert and I get into his car and he pulls away toward the highway. Through the window, I see the three brothers from Ninevah going back to their father's pickup truck. The older of Brown's boys is in the garage now, out of sight. Just as we pass, I look out to see his younger brother standing alone on the spot where we had been tossing washers. He is not grinning, and his eyes are no longer like saucers. They look, now, more like Bo's eyes.

Mr. Robert pulls the car onto the highway and drives past the Methodist church toward home. I don't look at the Nativity scene this time, as it slides past my window, but stare at the highway in front of us. There is a hollow feeling at the pit of my stomach and a lump in my throat. It is the same feeling that I had last summer after my father made me promise to wake him from his afternoon nap in plenty of time for us to get to town for the drawing held on Saturday mornings by local merchants. We had many tickets in the big metal lockbox that week and my father and I had carefully taped all of our stubs on sheets of cardboard so that we could quickly locate the winning number when it was called from the bank corner. When he came to find me, playing with Bo in the patch behind our house, it was midafternoon. I had forgotten to wake him and we missed the drawing. Since you had to be there to win, all of our stubs, so neatly taped in rows on the cardboard, were useless. He was angry, and disappointed, not so much in missing it, I think, as in me, for forgetting the time and effort that we had spent, together, in preparation for it. I ended up at the back of the well house, sulking. He came to find me, later, and told me that I should learn from this to pay better attention when told to do a thing. He also said that there would be other drawings. I quit pouting, but for several days after that the empty feeling would not go away.

I feel that way now, in the front seat with Mr. Robert. He is puffing away at his cigar, and the smoke from it seems especially rank in the close confines of the car. The heater is on too high, and I know that if I don't get out soon I will be sick. All Mr. Robert says, through the cloud of dingy smoke, is that he hopes Flossie has something good on the table for dinner. In Oakwood, we eat breakfast, dinner, and supper; lunch is an unheard-of undertaking.

When we get home, I tell Mr. Robert goodbye and run as fast as I can down the hill and through the gap in the hedge to our house, hoping to find Mother puttering around in the kitchen and the living room, rearranging the holly on the mantel or moving ornaments around on the tree, or decorating gingerbread men. I hope that she is doing Christmas things that will draw me into them, and away from the empty feeling.

She is, in fact, warming up a pot of leftover corn chowder for our dinner. Janie is still reading *Gone with the Wind* at the table. My father is in the back of the house somewhere.

"Back already?" Mother asks.

"We didn't stay long," I tell her as I survey the pies on the counter, ready for baking.

"Did you get to know Brown's boys?" she asks, stirring the chowder.

I am circling, with my fingertip, the ridge of dough around the potato pie. "I didn't get to *know* them," I say, pressing harder on the dough. "I just rode to town with 'em." Part of the dough breaks under my finger.

"Don't do that," she says, mashing the damp dough back into place. "What are their names?" she asks.

I push the pie away from me. "I don't *know*," I say, too loudly.

"What's gotten into you?" she asks, checking the pie for damage. "What are you so mad about?"

I can't tell her that I'm not mad at her, or at Brown's boys, or at the brothers from Ninevah, or at Mr. Robert for smoking up the hot car, or at myself for not even knowing Brown's boys' names. I'm mad at all of us. I'm mad because I have a hollow, sick feeling in my stomach on the best day of the year.

I start to cry.

"Good heavens!" my mother says, amazed. "I just asked you a simple question."

Janie, staring at all of this, shakes her head as if such is to be expected from the likes of me, and mutters, as she returns to her reading, something with the word "stupid" in it.

This does it. I turn on her and shout "Shut up!" before running out the back door, slamming it as hard as I can.

Bo is on his blanket in the well house and I hug him close to me, as if he's the last chance I have of being comforted. But when he lifts his sad eyes up to me, I can only see Brown's younger son, standing behind Greer Brothers, and the empty feeling stabs me.

After a while, my father comes into the well house and asks what the problem is. Mother has, no doubt, sent him out here, and Janie has probably told him I've lost my mind. He places a high value on anything Janie has to say, so I guess he thought he better come out here and check. His entrance starts me crying again, with renewed vigor. He looks at me for a minute or two before attempting several probes into the problem.

"Did something happen in town?" he asks. I shake my head no.

"Did somebody hurt your feelings?" No, again.

I can tell he is wondering how best to pursue this and, finally, he decides to come straight to the point.

"Then why are you behaving like this?" he asks. "Why did you yell at Janie?"

"I don't know," I tell him.

"Were Brown's boys mean to you?" he asks.

I shake my head from side to side, slinging tears on him and Bo.

"It don't matter about them," I tell him. "I'll never even see them again." I stroke Bo's back and he whimpers. "I don't even know their names." I sit still for a minute, sobbing, and neither of us talks. "They go to Dunbar," I say. "*You* don't ever even go over there, and you're the superintendent."

He takes this in, and rubs Bo behind his ears. "I don't go there because Mr. Oliver does a good job of running Dunbar," he says. "It would look wrong for me to go back and forth over there, making everybody believe I was running things."

I look at him for the first time.

"That would be wrong," he says. He leans down to touch my chin and holds it in a soft pinch. "Have you done something wrong?" he asks me.

And in one fell swoop, hardly stopping to take a breath, I tell him all of it: the flowerpots, the snowman, the washers, the brothers from Ninevah, Mr. Robert's hot car, and the pie dough.

He listens, and even seems to make some sense of it all. We sit quietly, when I'm done. He is silent for so long that I start to think it's about as likely for Bo to start talking as him.

"In a few years," he finally says, standing up straight to rub his back, "the schools will all be together." I've heard him and Mother talking of this before, and people in town. "Then there won't be a Dunbar." He begins to straighten Bo's blanket. "All the kids in town will go to one school. And things like this"—he points in the general direction of town—"won't happen as much." He rubs my close-cropped head with his palm. "But for now," he says, "you just have to handle things like that the best way you can." I look up at him, all cried out now. "You aren't happy with the way you handled it," he says. He takes a King Edward cigar out of his shirt pocket, unwraps it, licks one end, and, placing the damp end in his mouth, strikes a match and holds it to the other end. "But who's to say," he says, spitting little pieces of tobacco on the ground, "that you didn't do the best with it that you could."

"I didn't want to hurt their feelings," I tell him.

"I know you didn't," he says. When we are outside, he looks up the hill toward Miss Mae's backyard. "I'll tell you what," he says. "You pick out the best flowerpot in that bunch, and we'll plant something in it and Brown can take it home with him one day next week. I'll talk to Mae about it."

"You can't plant things this time of year," I tell him, much as I would explain something to Brown.

"Then we'll do it in the spring," he says. "Now come on in the house."

Walking behind him, I know that Diane, pretty in one of her turtlenecked sweaters, as pretty as I can imagine a person being, will soon be here with Lisa and Greg and Lynn. I know that, later, my father will drive to town on his annual shopping trip to Miss Tine's store. I know that Miss Mae will walk down the hill and through the gap in the hedge with her offerings for our tree; these she will call "remembrances, not gifts," but their lush wrappings and stickers which say "Neiman-Marcus" and "The Jay Shop" will tell us that they are very fine gifts indeed. I know that the packages that she will take away with her through the hedge won't have any stickers, since they came from the Sears, Roebuck catalog and were wrapped on the top of the deep freezer. I know that my father will keep the fire blazing, and that smoke will go up the chimney into the cold, starry night, and that Jimmy will make his way, under those stars, over country roads and highways, and that we will leave the tree lights on for him to see, and that Diane will be awake when he gets home. I know that Mother and I will look, for the last time today, at our tree, and that we will hold up and study our favorite ornament: a small, illuminated manger scene clamped snugly to a white bulb. I know that she will tell me to think, before I go to sleep tonight, of the real manger and of its precious promise, and that I will, in my bed, close my eyes and, seeing the plywood Nativity scene at the church and Annie Bell's house, try hard to see it. I know that when it is late and we are all in our beds, Lisa and Greg will stare at the window as Mother tells them to listen for reindeer bells. And I know that when all the town is asleep, except for me, I will know better, tonight, than to think that everyone in Oakwood is sleeping happily, or that they are all in the places where they should be.

t w o

August 1991   The frantic beats of three different songs spilled over from the girls' headphones into the van, providing a pulsating background to the classical station that Karen and I were listening to on the dashboard stereo. It reminded me of my ten years of driving a school bus to meets and tournaments when I had coached the high school tennis team. Then there had been over thirty individual headphones leaking out into the bus, and I always imagined what such massive volumes must be doing to the kids' eardrums, not to mention their brains.

Karen was dozing, and the girls were lost in their private blasts of music. I tapped on the cruise control, eased up the volume on Dvořák's *New World Symphony*, leaned back into the comfortable captain's seat, and watched the parched East Texas landscape glide by.

I used to wonder at men driving carloads such as this one when they would zip past me on the freeway, and I would imagine what it might be like to be in constant close association with that many people after so many years of living alone. Most of those years had been spent, of course, assuming that I would in fact marry and produce such a family. But, as the time slipped by, and each romance ran its course, I had begun to believe that my turn was not to come, and that teaching high school English, coaching the tennis team, catching Astros games with friends, reading, and taking student travel groups to Europe in the summers would have to be enough. I had even determined that it would be.

And then Karen had appeared. It was an arranged meeting: the recently divorced new elementary teacher and the confirmed bachelor high school coach. We met one October at a school conference and began to spend most of our free time together. I fell in love with Karen, and, in no particular order, with Kara, Haley, and Megan, her young daughters. We married on the afternoon of the last day of school in 1990 and I suddenly found myself in a house full of females (including their cat). And though much adjusting had been necessary, on all our parts (except, maybe, the cat's), it had been better than good. And now the man zipping by on the freeway was me.

Karen stretched and looked at the countryside. "Where are we?" she asked.

"Between Livingston and Lufkin."

She turned the air conditioner vent toward her, and watched a herd of thin cattle standing in a brown field. It was a scorching afternoon, cloudless and full of light. "We need to stop soon," she said. Megan, in second grade now and the youngest of the tribe, had already made her way to the front of the van to tell me this a few minutes before. This was one of the changes; in my bachelorhood I would drive great distances, hundreds of miles, before stopping. Now I gauged my journeys by rest rooms, not mileposts.

"Next gas station," I promised.

"Make it a McDonald's," Karen said. "I'm thirsty." A chorus of three "me, too"s came from the back. I was amazed that they could hear us through the pounding music.

I looked at the time on the dashboard. "Well, we'll have to make it a quick stop," I said. "I don't want Daddy to be alone too long."

Alene, my father's wife, was going to her grandson's wedding in Houston and would be away for several days. Janie had originally planned to stay with him but there had been a foul-up concerning the dates, and she and her husband, Thomas, were now with friends on the Mexican coast on a trip which had been booked for a long time. Karen and the girls and I were to stay the first two days and Diane would stay the last two. This seemed fair, since Janie visited him much more often than Diane or me. Diane was the office nurse for a doctor in Tyler, a long daily trip from her home on Lake Palestine, and I lived on the Gulf coast south of Houston.

Janie always had been our father's special protector, and he hers. They were kindred spirits. And lately, as he, who had always looked younger than his years, had become suddenly old before our eyes, Janie became even more diligent. She talked to him nearly every day on the phone, and, often, would call again, when she knew that he was taking a nap or sitting on the patio, to question Alene about his condition.

Now that he had begun to slip a bit (nothing serious, we told ourselves, and each other—just the occasional lapse of memory and short moments of confusion, the hesitation before taking a step and the hand cautiously touching the wall or the furniture as he ambled along—all to be expected at eighty-five), we had decided together that he should not be alone for four days.

We pulled into his and Alene's carport at midafternoon, and there he was, among a maze of hanging baskets full of trailing greenery and numerous wind chimes. He was sitting in a patio chair in his usual attire: freshly laundered slacks, a knit shirt, loafers, and a Dallas Cowboys cap. Whenever we came to see him, he was usually decked out in articles of clothing that we had given him. I never knew if this was his doing, or Alene's. I recognized the cap that we had brought on Father's Day, and the shirt that had been one of his Christmas presents.

As we climbed out of the van, he lifted himself, with great difficulty, out of his chair. He had to stand still a moment before coming toward us, as if to get his bearings, or to make sure that his legs were still working. It was obvious that he had been waiting for us.

"Right on time!" he said, tapping his watch. He always said this, though he never knew what time to expect us. The girls dutifully gave him hugs, though they hardly knew him, and Karen held his hands for a long time after their embrace. She asked him how he was and he said the inevitable "fine." In my entire lifetime I had never heard him give a different answer to this question, though he sometimes had reason enough to. We shook hands, and I squeezed his other arm lightly; this was as close as we had come to a hug since my childhood.

"You look good," I told him, and he said I did, too. A small stroke had left him blind in one eye a couple of years before, and he always squinted now, as if to better use the remaining eye, which had been weak for years. He gazed at me with the one remaining eye, like Brown used to do.

"Sit back down," I said. "I'll get our stuff in the house and we'll come out here and sit with you."

Instead, he turned and walked in his stiff, slow gait toward the back door. "I'll show you the layout," he said. I knew better than to protest. He gave every visitor the grand tour whether they needed it or not, so we all followed him in.

"This is the kitchen," he said, as he stopped to hold on to a chair at the breakfast table. "Are you hungry?" Megan, perpetually hungry, said that she was.

"We ate on the way," Karen said.

He took this in. "Well," he said, "there's plenty here. Make yourself at home." He thought for a moment. "Alene will be back in a little while and she'll make us some supper."

Karen and I looked at each other. I patted his shoulder as he made his way into the den.

"Alene left for Houston this morning, Daddy." He turned and looked at me. "Remember?" He nodded that he didn't. "She went down there with her family, to a wedding. We're going to stay here with you for a couple of days, and then Diane's coming to see you."

"Good," he said, tightening his lips into one of his thoughtful smiles. He was halfway through the den when he turned to look back at the kitchen. "Alene probably fixed some supper and left it for us," he said.

"We'll look later," Karen said. "Besides, we want to take you out to dinner."

He thought about this, and apparently decided that would be all right. "Good," he said. "I'll pay." He was, by nature, a provider. He had been raised in an era, and spent his career in a profession, in which money had been hard to come by. When I was growing up, he had kept an accurate account of all the household expenses; nothing very extravagant ever made its way into our house, except for some of the exotic ingredients needed for the recipes from my mother's cookbooks. It was important to him to pay his way. He didn't believe in credit cards, and always had a good bit of cash in his wallet.

We continued the tour.

"Here's the bathroom," he announced as he turned on the light. Opening a closet, he showed us the towels and washcloths. He even identified the tub for us. I thought he was about to point out the toilet and explain its function when a new thought occurred to him.

"Where will we all sleep?" he asked.

"We'll find a place," I told him. "You just take your regular bed."

"I can sleep on the couch," he said. Alene had told me that, lately, he took naps all through the day, so he probably logged more time on the couch than he did on his bed.

"You sleep in your bed," I told him. "We'll all have a place to sleep."

"Good." The thoughtful smile again.

We all stood in the hallway at the bathroom door, waiting for him to show us the rest of the house. He looked at each of us in turn. "I have to go in here," he said.

While he was in the bathroom, we moved off in several directions, like soldiers falling out of formation.

As I made my way through the back door with suitcases and totes, Karen showed me a note that Alene had left for us on the kitchen table. It said, in her pretty, flowing handwriting, that there was plenty of food in the refrigerator and cupboard and that we should make ourselves at home. What it did not say, but what Alene had told me on the phone the night before, was that my father had seemed more confused lately.

I glanced down the hall to make sure the bathroom door was still closed. "He seems worse," I said. Karen nodded that she thought so, too.

While Karen helped the girls get settled in, I took my own tour of the house, looking at the framed photographs on the walls and the knickknacks and mementos scattered around. How different this place was, I thought, from the house in Oakwood where I had grown up and where my father had spent so many years. Mother had not gone in for clutter, which is what she would have considered all these things arranged on tables and shelves. The one item which she would have been happy with was a large, built-in bookcase overflowing with hardbacks. Alene and I shared a love of murder mysteries, and I always enjoyed thumbing through her copies of Marsh, Christie, and other writers of whodunits. This is what I was doing when my father came out of the bathroom.

He paused at the entrance of the den and steadied himself with a walking stick that he had lifted from the umbrella holder in the hall. He looked at the walls and the ceiling for a moment, and then at me.

"That's a pretty cane you've got there," I said. I knew that Alene's son, a retired schoolteacher in Alto, had made it for him and had carved his initials into the handle. He had shown it to me on Father's Day.

"It helps me get around," he said. He looked at me again. I touched the rough, polished wood of the cane.

"Is this the one Terry Ted made for you?" I asked him.

He lifted the cane to inspect it. "I don't know," he said. "Alene got it somewhere." Kara, Haley, and Megan came into the room, having selected their beds and unpacked their clothes. He looked at them and smiled. "These are mighty pretty girls," he said, though it was obvious that he didn't know who they belonged to.

·   ·   ·

Later that night, after we had had dinner at a place that I remembered he liked, and Karen and the girls were inside watching a movie on television, we sat on the patio and sipped drinks. His longtime favorite was Old Crow with Sprite; I rattled the ice around in a glass of scotch and soda. It was a pretty summer night, and we sat quietly in the comfortable chairs and listened to insects buzzing near the lights. A soft breeze, full of the scents of honeysuckle and jasmine, worked through Alene's collection of wind chimes, and they sent out a tinkling song. Fireflies flashed on the dark lawn. I studied him as he watched them. He seemed so frail now, and much smaller than all of my best memories of him. His clothes seemed to hang on him, his thin arms and neck protruding from the bright blue shirt like the knobby wood of his cane.

"We'll go to bed when you're tired, Daddy," I said.

He continued to watch the fireflies. "I'm not tired."

After a few minutes, I tilted my glass in the direction of the lawn. The ice in my nearly empty drink clinked, joining in with the wind chimes. "Those lightning bugs remind me of Oakwood," I said.

He nodded, but he didn't seem to make the association.

"Do you remember when you would barbecue chickens outside and watch us chase the lightning bugs?" I asked him.

"I haven't cooked chickens in a long time," he said, taking a drink of his bourbon.

"Do you ever hear from anyone in Oakwood?" I asked.

He thought about it. "I don't think we have," he finally said. "Alene will know better than me." He looked into the darkness and then at his watch, though I was pretty sure he couldn't see it. "Shouldn't she be home by now?" he asked.

"Who?" I asked, still thinking about Oakwood.

He gave me a look that said that I should pay better attention to the conversation. "Alene," he said.

"She's in Houston," I said, trying to sound unsurprised. "Remember? She's at her grandson's wedding." He nodded that, yes, he seemed to remember that. "We're spending a couple of days with you and then Diane will be here."

"Good," he said, and smiled.

"Janie wanted to come, too," I said, "but she and Thomas are in Mexico on vacation."

"They are?" he said, brightening at the mention of Janie. "We went to Mexico City one time," he continued. "It was mighty pretty." I didn't know who he was speaking of; I was reasonably sure that I had never been to Mexico City. Sipping my drink, I thought it odd that he could recall a long-ago trip to Mexico and couldn't seem to remember where Alene was.

"I sure miss Oakwood," I said, trying to get him back on the subject that I most liked to visit with him about. It had been twelve years since he had married Alene and moved into her house in Longview. He had sold the house in Oakwood and the only times I ever saw it were when, stopping to visit Miss Mae on the way to somewhere else, I would stand in her driveway and look down the hill, over the hedge, at the place that held so many memories.

"I used to live in Oakwood," he said, matter-of-factly. I nearly dropped my drink.

I managed to say, "You lived there a long time."

He nodded.

"You spent many a year in the Oakwood school, didn't you?" I asked.

He nodded again.

"We'll have to go down there one of these days, you and I," I said. His smile seemed to say that he liked the idea. "I haven't been down there since the old school burned."

"It didn't all burn down," he said, taking another drink from his glass. "They just had to rebuild the insides." I knew that he was thinking of the first time the school burned, in the late forties, when Diane had been in grade school.

I sat forward in my chair, to be closer to him. "But it burned again, Daddy. Just a few years ago." He looked as if it was news to him. "Don't you remember? It was about the same time that Old Main at Sam Houston burned down," I continued. "You've seen the new school. They had a big reunion and you and Alene went." He just stared at me. "You were the guest of honor."

He nodded that he remembered, but I could tell that he didn't.

"We'll go down there," I said. "There are lots of folks who would like to see you."

"Anytime you say," he said, draining his glass. We sat in silence for quite a while and he stared at the carport.

"Where's my car?" he finally asked.

"Alene drove it to Terry Ted's," I told him. "They went to Houston."

He thought about it. "I have a son who teaches school somewhere down around Houston," he said.

When the girls were in bed, and my father, having looked out the window, had asked me, twice more, where his car was, I lay in bed with Karen and told her of the strange conversation on the patio. She said that Alene's absence had probably brought all this on. After all, he depended on her, these days, for everything.

We left our bedroom door open so that we could hear him if he got up during the night. I had looked in his room before I went to bed and he had been sound asleep, snoring like he did in the old days.

"I'm worried about him," I said, not able to stay interested in the Agatha Christie novel I had pilfered from Alene's bookshelf. "I don't know how long he'll be able to stay here, or how long Alene will be able to take care of him."

"Maybe he just had a bad day," Karen said.

I turned off the reading light. "I'm pretty sure he thinks I stole his car," I said before going to sleep.

Late in the night, Karen woke me up and told me that he had gone into the bathroom and had been there a long time. I tapped on the bathroom door and asked if he was all right.

He opened the door and looked at me a moment before speaking. "I can't find Alene," he said. I told him, again, about her trip and that we were staying with him. He clinched his lips into his familiar half smile. "Good," he said.

"Let's go to bed now," I suggested.

And my father touched my arm. "Now, tell me again," he said. "Who are you?"

three

It is a warm May morning near the end of my eighth-grade year. In less than two weeks, I will march with the other members of my small class across the stage of the school's auditorium to receive, from my father, a diploma attesting to my completion of junior high school. The graduating seniors, all nine of them, will be sitting on the stage with the members of the school board, my father, and a couple of local preachers recruited to offer up prayers of thanksgiving for the seniors' accomplishments, and to invoke blessings for their futures.

It is Wednesday. The windows in the classroom in which I am sitting are all open, but there is no breeze outside, so it's as hot in here as it is out there. Mr. Jacobs is telling us a story about his Army days on a hot military post in West Texas. The sandstorms were so bad there, he tells us, that it was impossible to keep sand out of the food, and clothes, and bunks. We all shift and twitch at our desks, feeling and tasting the sand. The heat is easy to imagine, since it must be over eighty degrees in here.

This is history class, but Mr. Jacobs, a born storyteller,

is easily led astray from our textbook, especially this late in the year. He is a tall man with a burr haircut, even shorter than my father's crew cut. Most of the boys in my class, including myself, have graduated from crew cuts to longer hairstyles which involve parting and combing. Butch Wax, the pink concoction which kept our bristles at attention, has given way to Brylcreem. Mr. Jacobs's hair is too close-cropped for even Butch Wax.

He was a good baseball player at Sam Houston State, but an electrical accident resulted in the amputation of his right arm just below the elbow. It doesn't slow him down any as a teacher and baseball coach; when giving fielding practice, he rests the bat in his clinched nub, tosses the ball high in front of him, and, in the quickest motion any of us has ever seen, grabs the handle of the bat and hits the ball to any player he chooses. He drives a standard-shift pickup truck by steadying the wheel with his nub as he finds the gears with his left hand. He even mows yards for extra income in the summer, and the sight of him quickly pushing his old mower with his remaining arm is common to everyone in Oakwood.

Mr. Jacobs does everything fast. It's hard to carry on a conversation with him as he walks down the hall or out to the baseball field; he moves so swiftly that it seems that he will break into a run at any moment. In the classroom, he moves constantly, waving his half arm in the air to emphasize whatever point he is making. He also talks fast, and, when he gets excited, his words sound as though they were being shot from an automatic rifle.

He is rattling on about the sand in his bunk when my father knocks on the classroom door and asks if he can borrow a couple of boys for a few minutes. Everyone is ready to volunteer, but Jim Bob and I are the quickest. Mr. Jacobs, always impressed with quickness, points to us with his nub and resumes his story.

We follow my father down the hall to his office. Miss Laura June, his secretary, smiles at us as we go by her desk. My father points to the film projector in his office and the bundles of electrical cords on top of the row of four file cabinets, and tells us to gather these up for the movie assembly. Grades one through twelve gather in the auditorium every Wednesday morning during the last two months of school and watch a film that my father has ordered from a rental company in Dallas. Usually, we see documentaries about the various states, but sometimes he shows us a feature film. He is big on the Francis (the Talking Mule) and the Ma and Pa Kettle series. Jim Bob and I strain to read the label on the metal film canister on the desk, hoping for one of these; we frown when we see that it is *Hawaii: Jewel of the Pacific*.

We busy ourselves with gathering up the projector, cords, and film. My father tells us to take them down to the stage and wait for him, then he steps through the open side door of his office into the classroom in which he teaches math and typing. The slow tapping of the heavy Royal manual typewriters increases to a brisk rhythm when he enters. He commands a good bit of respect around here and in the town. Since I'm not in high school yet, I haven't had him as a teacher. But both Diane and

Janie did, and both said that they just kept their mouths shut and tried hard not to call attention to the relationship. It's hard to imagine Janie being anxious, since, at home, he would paint the house pink if she asked him to.

At the front of the auditorium, Jim Bob and I sit on the edge of the stage and wait for him.

"I wish he would get some real movies," Jim Bob says. I nod in agreement. Several times, I have studied the film catalog in the office and made suggestions—maybe a Western or a good war story—but my father seems intent on travelogues and hillbillies and talking mules. "It's still better than being in class," Jim Bob reasons.

When he arrives, we help him set up the projector on a typing table in the center aisle and run the cords down to the front. While he threads the film through the machine, we find the portable screen in a storage closet and wrestle it into position on the stage. "Don't step on those lights," he tells us. He is particularly protective of these footlights, since Mr. Stake, a county music teacher of several years ago, always broke some of them on each of his weekly visits. Mr. Stake was very dramatic and, when giving his lessons, would flail and hop around with the music. Many such hops landed on the lightbulbs in their sunken trench at the edge of the stage. My father could never see why a grown man would be jumping around in the first place, but since Mr. Stake worked for the county superintendent, he had no authority over him. Ever thrifty, he finally told Mr. Johnson, the custodian, to remove all the bulbs on the days of the music lessons.

I failed miserably at this enrichment. Mr. Stake tried

me on every instrument before determining that I was just not musically inclined. Janie, however, then still in high school, was one of his best pupils. She took up the accordion with great fervor, and my parents and I spent many tortured hours as she coaxed "Beer Barrel Polka" and other delights from the huge, gasping thing. But for Janie, all of us were relieved when the county superintendent dropped the music program, and Mr. Stake moved on to other musical adventures. Mr. Johnson was, no doubt, happier than anybody, since he wouldn't have to constantly remove and replace all those bulbs in the footlights.

When we are finished with the chore, my father sends us back to class, where Mr. Jacobs is moving briskly around the room, telling how the siege of the Alamo would have ended much differently had the defenders had modern weapons of the type that he had used when in the Army on that post in West Texas. B. D. Owens asks him if the Mexicans wouldn't have had modern weapons, too. While Mr. Jacobs ponders this, Chris Stevens, whispering, asks me what the movie is for today. He doesn't look particularly happy when I tell him.

Later, we are all sitting in the auditorium waiting for the film to start. My father is big on assemblies, so we have them pretty often. Sometimes, the elementary classes present programs full of dancing and recitations and the wearing of bright hats and costumes, and local people come every once in a while to inspire us to do well in our studies. Mr. Nubbin Eldridge speaks to us at least once a year; he is a natural orator, and will give the commencement address in a couple of weeks. Once a year, my father hires Mr. Gunn, a magician from Jacksonville, to put on a magic show. I watched my father write Mr. Gunn a check, on the school account, for his performance last year. The magician folded the check and asked why he didn't just have the students pay a quarter each, as many schools did. "Because a lot of them don't have a quarter," my father told him, "and if anybody sees a show here, everybody sees it." Several years ago, the entire school, all twelve grades, had gone on three school buses to Buffalo to watch John Wayne's *The Alamo* at the Rio Theater. He had written a check that day, too. It was the first time that some of the kids had seen a motion picture in a movie theater.

My father walks to the front of the stage and leads us in the Pledge of Allegiance. Then he tells us that today's film is about Hawaii, which he pronounces "Hiwahya." "I once won a free vacation there," he tells us. Everyone looks impressed, and my friends look at me, wondering why I have never mentioned it. "I was sent there by Uncle Sam during the war," he says. This brings polite laughter from everyone. My father always brags about our behavior and attentiveness during assemblies. It is, of course, due partly to fear of reprisal; anyone foolish enough to misbehave will be sternly corrected from the stage, or, if my father feels that the disruption warrants it, he will point to a teacher to remove the transgressor to the office, to wait with Miss Laura June until my father can remedy the situation with the long, slender paddle he keeps in his desk. Oakwood is a country town, and the people here are in favor of instilling good behavior in youth at all costs. My father is highly respected by the parents—he taught most of them when they had gone to school—and they rarely question his judgment.

One of the teachers turns on the projector, and another flips off the lights in the auditorium. After a moment of static from the single speaker, a test pattern comes on the screen and we are soon taken to the lush, splashy colors of Hawaii: jewel of the Pacific. The scene pans from Diamond Head to a white sand beach. Hawaiian music plays and the deep-voiced narrator asks us if we have ever dreamed of palm trees swaying in a gentle tropical breeze beside a dark, blue sea. Some Hawaiian children, brown and smiling, run along the edge of the water in skimpy, colorful attire.

"They look like niggers," someone behind me whispers. There is a chorus of giggles. "It'll look like that around here next year," someone else says in a low voice. Mr. Snyder, two rows in front of us, rotates his wide head, as large as a basketball and as close-sheared as Mr. Jacobs's, on his thick neck and glares in our direction. All is quiet. We watch as rows of sugarcane sweep by on the screen and listen to the narrator tell us of that crop's importance to the state's economy.

The Oakwood schools will be integrated next year or the year after. It has been the foremost topic of discussion in town and at school for some time now; no one seems happy about it, and everyone blames the government.

Much is said about the Supreme Court having too much power, and President Johnson, a Texan and a Democrat, two cardinal virtues in the town's opinion, is much lambasted for having forgotten his roots. I've noticed that my father has little to say on the issue. He has called more school board meetings than usual, and has spent more of his time at Dunbar, the black school, talking with Professor Oliver.

I still think about Brown's sons, and of that day beside Greer Brothers'. Brown and I don't see as much of each other as we used to, but he is still there at Miss Mae's. We wave at each other over the hedge sometimes, and we visit occasionally. But I don't eat his fried hot water corn bread anymore, while he sits on his upturned bucket and has his lunch under one of Miss Mae's trees. He has never mentioned his sons, and I've never asked. I never knew their names. They'll be in school here after integration; I wonder if they'll know me.

After the narrator bids aloha to Hawaii, the last of the film runs through the projector and flaps on the take-up reel before a teacher turns the machine off. The lights come on, and everyone is released back to class. The elementary grades leave first, and we watch them file up the aisle like ducks behind their teachers, an assortment of ladies known by their first names prefaced by "Miss." The junior high and high school students and teachers follow them out, and Jim Bob and I rewind the film and put the gear away. By the time we get to class, the morning is over.

As we file past Miss Laura June in the lunchroom to

get our tickets punched, someone ahead of me says, "I reckon they'll be serving possum and watermelon eveh day next year." Someone else says, "I won't be eatin' with 'em. My daddy, he says for me to sit at a plumb different table." There are several murmurs of agreement.

"Hush up there," Miss Laura June says, snapping her card puncher twice to emphasize the point.

We move down the line, and the lunch ladies put generous portions of meat loaf, mashed potatoes, green beans, and peach cobbler on our metal trays. My father waits until everyone is served, then takes his tray and sits at his regular place at the teachers' table.

When we've finished eating, and have scraped the remaining food from our trays into the garbage cans at the end of the kitchen, Jim Bob and Chris and B. D. and I hurry to the big open area behind the school where a daily game of work-up softball is played. The first three to get there get to bat, the next one to arrive is the catcher, and the next four fill in the infield positions. Everyone else takes a place in the outfield. On some days, there are so many outfielders that it's hard to find a place to stand. Mr. Jacobs is always the pitcher. The batters get to keep their status until they are either struck or tagged out, then everyone moves up a position. The numerous outfielders have only one chance to bat; if someone catches a fly ball, he or she takes the place of the batter. Almost everyone in the junior high and high school takes part every day, and the game continues until the bell rings for fourth period. The lunch ladies have complained to my father that anticipation of this activity makes everyone eat too fast; whether their concern has to do with the students' digestion or their lack of proper appreciation of the meal is unclear. So far, he has allowed the game to continue.

The afternoon passes slowly, and finally it is three-thirty and the last bell rings. The kids who live nearby head off toward home, wandering in groups along the narrow street that leads to town. Those who live in the country climb on school buses. I always go to the classroom beside my father's office to do my homework until he is ready to go home. Today, he is having a faculty meeting in there, so I sit down at his desk to do my lessons. The surface of the desk is in its usual state of perfect order; stacks of letters and bills, anchored by paperweights, are straight and parallel to each other; freshly sharpened pencils stand ready for use in a leather holder; a Webster's dictionary and a Texas almanac rest between metal bookends. I spread out my math book and paper and begin working the problems that are due tomorrow.

Through the closed door that connects the office to the classroom, I can hear the teachers scraping the chairs around on the concrete floor, taking their places at the typing tables. Miss Laura June is typing in her office, so it's hard for me to hear what is going on in the meeting, but I follow the general progress in bits and pieces. My father goes over procedures pertaining to the end of the school year, like grade reporting, textbook collections, and storage of materials for the summer. There is much discussion about something; I can't tell what. Several teachers are speaking at once, and then just a couple, and then just my father.

Miss Laura June has gone home now and I am through with my homework. I pick up the copy of *King Solomon's Mines* that I checked out from the library today and am about to start reading it when I notice that it's gotten awfully quiet in the meeting. I know that they haven't finished, for there would be a great scraping of chairs and cackle of voices. I swivel around in the wooden desk chair and listen intently.

After another few moments of silence, my father speaks. He has obviously taken his time formulating the correct answer to an important question, and I move quietly to the door to hear it.

"It looks like there won't be total integration for at least another year," he says. There seems to be a collective sigh of relief among the teachers. He waits until it is completely quiet before he continues. "Next year, it will be on a voluntary basis." I can hear him walking. He is probably stepping closer to a window, to see if there is any breeze at all in the hot afternoon. I move back toward the desk, half afraid that he will come sweeping in and present me to the faculty as an example of someone who listens at closed doors.

When he continues walking, I resume my eavesdropping position. "And Mr. Oliver tells me that there are several students at Dunbar who want to come here." There is much mumbling and scooting of chairs at this, and my father waits until it has died down.

"Can't Professor Oliver advise them not to do it?" someone asks. A few teachers agree that this would be a good idea.

It is quiet again, and I know that my father is choosing his next words with great care.

"In the first place," he finally says, "I don't intend to ask him to do that. He's told me that the students who have volunteered to come are not troublemakers, and they haven't been put up to this by anyone." He pauses. "And in the second place, and I want to be mighty clear on this, when they come, whether it's all of them or just a few, it's our job to make them feel welcome, and to treat them just like we do any other student." No one says anything; no chairs scrape. "I know there will be difficulties," he continues. "Change is hard. I have as much trouble with it as any of you." He waits a moment before adding, "But change is coming, and it's our job to make it as easy on everyone as we can." He pauses before continuing. "I'm a lot closer to retirement than the rest of you," he tells them. "So it'll be your problem soon." There is some nervous laughter. "My best advice is to not let it be a problem."

The telephone rings and I tell the caller that my father is in a teachers' meeting. As I hang up, I can hear the chairs scraping away from the tables and know that it is over. He comes into the office and asks if I finished my homework. He sits at the desk and begins reading the letters that Miss Laura June left for him to sign.

Later, when all the teachers are gone, and just the two

of us are left in the building, he makes sure that everything is neat on the desk and in the long middle drawer and takes his ring of keys out of his pocket. Finding the smallest key, he checks one last time to see that everything is in its place before locking the desk. Then he locks the three file cabinets which contain the official school records and transcripts, and now he closes the heavy door of the safe in the corner, twirling the combination and giving two yanks on the handle.

Outside, we lower the American flag from the pole and he folds it carefully into a tight bundle and takes it into the office before locking the door.

When we are in the school car, an olive drab military staff car bought at the government surplus store in Longview, he takes a last look at the long red-brick building. It is old now, and, in the light of most educational standards, outdated. But he watched it being built, and then watched it being rebuilt, after the fire. It is part of him. And I know that his retirement is on his mind a lot these days. He has no hobbies, nor any significant or time-consuming interests other than us and his work. I can't imagine him not going to his job every day.

When he leaves, it won't be because of integration. He knows that when it comes, the town, both white and black, will mumble a little while, and then just do it. An old friend of his has pulled some strings, and arranged for him to be offered a job in central Texas. I've heard him talking to Mother about it, and I know that it will be some kind of political appointment, in one of President

Johnson's "Great Society" programs. If he takes it, he'll be the director of something or other for some county. It's bound to pay more money than his superintendent's job, or he wouldn't leave it.

When he is through looking at the school, and is satisfied that everything's all right, he starts the car, and we head for home.

We always drive with the windows open, since there is no air conditioner. I'm not sure if the radio works; I can't remember anyone ever turning it on. We turn off the school road and make our way along some short dirt roads, with white wood frame houses on either side. The houses all have wide porches, and the porches all have chairs or hanging swings on them. Most of the houses have air conditioner units emerging from one of the windows, like ugly growths on the sides of cattle. Everybody has screens on their open windows and doors, to protect against the mosquitoes, which aren't too bad usually, and the dust from the road, which is always thick.

Soon, we are on the long dirt road which runs parallel to the highway. We leave a cloud of red dust behind us like waves in the wake of a boat. My father notices the copy of *King Solomon's Mines* that I am holding.

"Are you reading that for English class?" he asks me.

"No," I tell him, "I'm just reading it."

"Good," he says, shifting the old car into a lower gear to make the turn into the narrow lane that runs beside the edge of Miss Mae's property out to the highway. He asks if I liked the film today, and I tell him I did, wondering if now would be a good time to mention that we would all sure enjoy a real movie next week.

"I'd like to go back to Hawaii [Hiwahya] someday," he says as we bounce along the little lane beside Miss Mae's property. "Maybe you can take me when you're rich."

Uncle Gaston's car is in our driveway when we get home. My father and I both smile when we see it. Uncle Gaston is my father's brother and is a salesman for a furniture company in Dallas. Every six weeks or so, always on Wednesday, he spends the night with us on his way to Palestine and other towns in East Texas to call on furniture stores. He is a great favorite in our house, and we all look forward to his visits.

He is sitting at the kitchen table, smoking a cigarette and visiting with my mother, who is cooking supper. Uncle Gaston is tall and slender, his shock of snow-white hair always in need of combing, and his huge red nose, common to Rozelles, is the dominant feature on his wrinkled face. He is several years older than my father, certainly old enough to have retired long ago, but he enjoys the life of a traveling salesman, taking as much delight in the visits to his regular stores—and the people who work there and are happy to see him, and laugh at his jokes— as he does in returning to Dallas and Aunt Billie.

"Hello, Johnnie," he says as I enter. He talks loud.

"Ronnie," I correct him. He knows my name; this is our private joke. He erupts into one of his wheezy laughs. Uncle Gaston has an asthmatic voice, full of loud intakes and output of breath, and, even when he is quiet, his heavy breathing sounds like a bellows being pumped. His dentures smack and click as he takes in great gulps of air. I sometimes wonder if this constant rattling has something to do with the size of his nose.

"Hello, Lester," he wheezes, rising to shake my father's hand. He asks him if he had a nice drive down from Dallas.

"It's always a nice drive when it ends up at one of Quinda's suppers," Uncle Gaston says, before seeming to suck the words back in again.

My mother smiles at this, and tells my father to make Uncle Gaston a drink. "He'll never take one till you get home," she says.

My father takes down the bottle of Old Crow and begins mixing it with soda in two glasses. The only time he drinks during the week is when Uncle Gaston visits.

My mother continues preparing our supper while the two brothers sit at the table and visit over their drinks. They have loosened their neckties and lean back comfortably in their chairs, happy to see each other.

In my room, I hurriedly go about putting my school things away, anxious to join the festivities in the kitchen. I can hear them in there; my father is laughing, and Uncle Gaston snorts and wheezes.

I hear Mother coughing in the hall. I know that she is coming to call my attention to something that I've done wrong. Conversation between us these days seems to be limited to my failings. Mother feels bad most of the time.

She has been in and out of hospitals in Houston and Temple for tests; they've all told her to quit smoking, and she's brought home more pills to take from each place. My father says it's her nerves that are the problem, and he seems to be able to tolerate her dark moods better than I can.

"You didn't make your bed this morning," she says from my doorway. I look at the perfectly made bed.

"I was running late," I tell her.

"So I'm supposed to make it because you were running late?"

"You didn't have to make it," I say. "I would have made it when I got home."

"Why should it be a mess just because you forgot to do it?" she asks.

I wonder if she is enjoying this; maybe she's looked forward to it all day. "I didn't forget to do it," I say. "I told you I didn't have time to do it."

She gives me the resigned look that I have come to dread and that I get from her more and more often; it's a mixture of disappointment and disgust. "But I do have time?" she asks. "Is that it?"

"I'll do it from now on," I tell her, ready to be done with it.

"We'll see," she says as she turns to go back to the kitchen. I hear her tell my father and Uncle Gaston that supper is ready and that she is going to lie down for a while. When I get to the kitchen, my father is serving the plates.

During the meal, Uncle Gaston says that Mother seems tired, and asks how she is doing.

"About the same," my father says, not looking up from his supper.

Later, after the table has been cleared of dishes, Uncle Gaston, clacking the ice around in another drink, tells story after story about life on the road. They are all funny, and I laugh as he wheezes and snorts his way through them. My father laughs, too, but not as much as he usually does, and he glances every so often toward the back bedroom. He knew, when Mother said that she was going to lie down for a while, that she wouldn't be back. He knew that she had taken a bunch of her pills so that she could just go to sleep and forget about the pain and misery that she was feeling. He goes, a couple of times, to check on her.

With every sip of his Old Crow, Uncle Gaston's nose seems to take on a deeper hue of red, and his dentures clack loudly when he laughs and sucks in big gulps of air. He looks at his watch, and tells us that he has an early call at Palestine.

I help my father clean up the kitchen while Uncle Gaston gets ready for bed. I think I can hear his loud breathing from the bathroom. My father is washing dishes and pans at the sink; I stand beside him, drying each one as he hands it to me. We work at it quietly for a few minutes.

"Did you and your mother have an argument?" he asks, taking his time with a roasting pan, scrubbing it till it shines in the dull light over the sink.

"She jumped all over me for not making my bed," I tell him. "She made a big deal out of it."

He continues his slow assault on the pan. "The house *is* a big deal to her," he says. "You know that."

"It's not like I did it on purpose," I say. "I didn't have time to do it this morning." Not having a dish to dry at the moment, I rub at my hands with the towel, to have something to do other than looking at him. "It's just a bed," I say, "and she had to go and make such a big thing out of it, and go to bed and miss Uncle Gaston." I take the pan from him and begin to dry it. "She used to look forward to him coming, too."

He is through with the dishes now, and drains the water from the sink. "Your mother feels bad," he says, wiping his hands with the dishtowel. "Little things upset her." He carefully folds the cloth and hangs it on the towel rack beside the sink.

I don't look up from the pan that I'm drying. "She always feels bad," I say.

"She doesn't want it that way any more than we do," he says. He looks at me; I can see how tired he is, from the long day at school, from the visit with Uncle Gaston, and from worrying about my mother. I know that he misses Janie, who is married now and lives in Huntsville with her husband, Thomas, the first and only boy that she ever dated, and their baby. Thomas is in college at Sam Houston.

My father turns off the lights. "It's awfully easy to get mad at your mother because she's sick," he tells me as I move toward my room. "I do it, too." We look at each other across the room. "We've got to remember that she feels bad, and try to make her happy."

"I know," I say, looking at the floor.

As I pass the open door to Janie's old room, I lean in and tell Uncle Gaston I'll see him at breakfast. "Good night, Johnnie," he snorts and clacks from the bed.

Later, getting ready for bed, I hear Uncle Gaston's labored snoring, as loud as Janie's renditions on the accordion, competing with the rumbling attic fan as it churns away over the hallway. I know that my father is lying awake in his bed at the back of the house, alone with his problems, one of which he faces for the entire town and about which he can do nothing less than make the best of it. He knows that integration is right, and he knows that it is coming. But he also knows that it will travel a long, hard road before it will be accepted. He has to make up his mind about the job in central Texas. He is a schoolteacher; it's all he's ever done, and it's all that he ever wanted to do. How will he feel without a school to run and classes to teach? He has never been political, even with the various school boards who gave him his contracts through the years, and this job looks awfully political to me.

I think he's also a little worried about how the town will feel about his pulling up stakes and leaving, especially right now, when this big change is about to happen. He's never done a cowardly or an irresponsible thing that I know of, and he probably figures that some people will see this as one. Sometimes I worry about how he is seen by other people, like my friends. He's the superintendent, so sometimes, when a particular school rule threatens or hinders one of my friends, I imagine him looking at me, thinking that my father sat down at his desk one day and thought up all the rules just to aggravate all of us. He is different from the fathers of my friends. He's older, in the first place, and he doesn't sell things in a store or raise cattle or grow crops. He doesn't hunt or fish; sometimes I think he may be the only male, man or boy, in Oakwood who doesn't. And now he may be going off to work for Lyndon Johnson, whose popularity has gone steadily downhill in his native state.

His other problem lies sleeping beside him. This will be another difficult and painful road, leading who knows where.

With every problem he faces, I seem to know my father better. And with every passing day of my mother's dark metamorphosis, I don't seem to know her at all.

four

August 1991   Karen and the girls and I were in our new house. It was before sunrise, and even before the local and the Houston papers plopped into our driveway. I was sitting in my study, which had been a dining room for the family that had sold us the house. I had always wanted one, ever since I saw *Leave It to Beaver* when I was little. Ward Cleaver had a dandy study, though I was never sure what it was that he did in there, besides impart wisdom to Beaver and Wally. My father never had one, so I suppose his office at the school served to satisfy whatever craving he had in that regard.

Bookcases lined one wall of mine, and all my treasures, my Hemingways and Faulkners, my mysteries, the guidebooks and histories that I had bought at Canterbury, and Versailles, and Mount Vernon, and countless other places, rested in rows in their new home. A few of the novels that had been in my mother's bookshop, in the front room of my grandparents' big house before she married my father, were there. The first mystery that I ever read was there. It was *The Yellow Room* by Mary Roberts Rinehart; it had come from Mother's shop, and I had read it when I was twelve. When I looked at it, small and stained and not very impressive among several bigger and newer volumes, it was like seeing a crinkled photograph of a first love.

Karen and the girls were sound asleep. After I made the coffee, I looked out the window in our den and saw the cat, dozing on the redwood swing on the patio. After just a week, she was already at home here, as we all were. Though moving had been hectic, we felt, when it was over, that we had ended up where we were supposed to be in the first place.

There was a large window over my desk that looked out over the entryway of our house. The little open area that led up to our front door was full of plants—hawthorns and ivy and Mexican heather—and tall schefflera in pots. The leaves and vines wandered around along the ground and on the bricks of the house. I could imagine sitting at that desk and writing fine novels that would win critical acclaim and send the girls to college and Karen and me to an early retirement. I had no idea what the novels would be about, but I figured if I sat there enough hours of enough days, looking at the plants in the entryway, something would come to me.

It was a good feeling, that early morning, to be the only one awake, my family safe and sleeping in a new house. The mug of coffee was warm in my hand, and the very first hint of pink sunlight was filtering through the big trees that I could see around the edge of the entryway.

Soon, birds would be singing, and Karen and I would get ready for work. The girls had another couple of days of summer before their school year began; we were still in faculty meetings.

The day before, Karen and Megan, the youngest of the three girls, and I had walked the little trail that led from our subdivision to the elementary school that Megan would now be attending. She was a precise and ordered child, traits she shared with my father, and she wanted no surprises; for Megan, everything had to be in its proper place, where she expected it to be. She would be walking to school every day, and intended to learn all that she could about it before she actually had to go on her own. So we stopped many times on that little journey, and looked at yards that might have dogs, and inclines that might be slick in damp weather. When we visited Janie's house in the summer, or went on vacation, Megan would lay out her clothes for the trip, in sets, with matching underwear and socks, long before our departure. Her suitcase, zipped up and ready to go, stood by her door for perhaps a week before it was needed. My father was just like that, methodical and controlled, at least he had been once.

Janie had called a couple of days before to tell me that he was sick. He had a bad cold, or maybe the flu, and she said that his illness made him even more confused than usual. Since our visit, earlier that month, he had been on my mind, stepping in every once in a while, out of no-where, when I would be thinking about something else.

I had talked to Alene about his recent behavior, and she said that he had good days and bad. I told her that the ones that we had spent with him must have fallen into the bad variety.

Janie went on to say that he was awfully weak from his bout with whatever it was that he had, and that it seemed to drain what fragile memory he had left. He seemed to be in a fog right now, denser than the one he was wandering through when I had last seen him. I told her I would call Alene to check on him, and asked if she thought I needed to go up there. She knew that we had just settled into the new house, and that our school year was just beginning—so was hers; she taught elementary school, like Karen—and suggested we not go yet. We may all have to go soon enough, she said.

After her call, all I could think about was Alzheimer's disease. I had never even heard of it until a few years before, but now everybody seemed to have it. During one of our faculty meetings, while my colleagues did lesson plans or worked crossword puzzles, I read about Alzheimer's in a book I found in the school library. I learned that not only was there no cure for it, the medical community hadn't even come to a consensus as to what caused it. Often, the book told me, old people started forgetting things, and, in due course, were diagnosed with Alzheimer's. From there, the progression went, almost always, slowly and sadly downhill.

My father had forgotten many things, and, it seemed, some people. Like me, for instance.

Being misplaced by a parent was a hard thing, but an even harder one was having to watch someone who had always been so resolutely in charge of things suddenly lose that control, and drift, now, in currents not of his planning, or even of his knowledge.

He had always been a predictable man, driven by routine. Before he went to bed each night, he laid out all the objects from his pockets—his handkerchief, wallet, coins (stacked by value), penknife, pens, and pocket comb—in precise order on his dresser. He must have been a whiz at passing inspections in the Army.

Very rarely did he stray from his routines, and do something sudden or surprising. Once, when my sister Diane and her husband, Jimmy, spent a summer in Florida while Jimmy worked on a pipeline, they took Janie, then in the seventh or eighth grade, with them. My father came home from work one day, about three weeks into their trip, and sat down to the dinner that Mother had made. It was a hot late June day, and he ate almost half of his meal before announcing, almost as an afterthought, that he intended to buy a new car that afternoon and that the three of us would leave in it, in a couple of days, to drive to Florida to see the rest of the family and have a nice vacation. When he had finished, he turned his attention back to his meal, and Mother and I looked at each other to confirm that we had heard everything correctly.

A holiday of this magnitude, from a man who had never provided one loftier than two days in Galveston, was startling, to say the least. He wouldn't have surprised us more if he had said that he had booked passage for us on a Mercury rocket like the one John Glenn had just ridden into space. Of course, looking back on it later, we all knew why he did it. He missed Janie. But Mother and I got a fine trip out of it; we loaded up in a brand-new Chevy Impala and I ventured over the Texas state line for the first time in my life.

His purchase of our lake house, a small wood frame structure built on stilts, was also uncharacteristic. He bought it even before I was born, I think, and nobody ever really knew why. He liked to go there and cook chickens on the grill, but chickens could have been cooked on the grill in the backyard, in town. It was a curious extravagance, since he didn't hunt or fish, the two best reasons for having a place like that. But he had bought it, and paid his yearly dues to the Taylor Fishing Club (which owned the private lake) and never, to my knowledge, wet a hook in that lake or any other. He enjoyed cooking what my friends and I caught out of it. And he liked having his buddies from town, or sometimes the superintendents from other schools, come down there to play poker. My mother liked to sit in a wooden rocker, which she had painted orange, on the screened-in porch and watch the lake in its many moods.

It was called Stanmire, and was a long, narrow body of greenish-brown water that was once part of the Trinity River. There were no houses on one side of the lake, since the river, a short distance through the trees, sometimes, during the spring rains, left its new channel in search of its old one. It was a pretty lake, with plenty of tall trees on the shore, draped with long, intricate strands of gray Spanish moss, hanging like jewels on rich old women. There was good fishing there all the year, perch and bass in special places and blue channel catfish along the bottom. Multitudes of frogs could be had by anyone wanting them, or with the time or inclination to go and gig them. Snakes, mostly cottonmouth moccasins, and snapping turtles were also in abundance. The snakes' and turtles' heads were common sights gliding slowly along out in the lake, their narrow wakes as straight as rulers behind them. Stanmire gave its best to us, and we took it; everybody enjoyed what it had to offer. My father seemed content just providing it for the rest of us. It was enough, for him, to cook big platters of chickens while we all played or fished, or to sit on the long porch and watch while his children and grandchildren swam out past the end of the pier.

The trip to Florida and the purchase of the lake house were exceptions to an otherwise utterly predictable life. It had been just such deviations that had first called our attention to the initial stages of his current dilemma.

Alene had been having some tests run in the local hospital, and he was sitting in the waiting area with Alene's son, the retired schoolteacher, and her daughter. Alene was still in the examination room, and the little group in the waiting area had been told that the doctor would be out to give them the results of the tests at any moment. Suddenly, my father stood up, told no one in particular that he needed a watch, and left the room. Alene's son and daughter both assumed that he had left his watch in the car, or that he might just want to get out of the sterile, cold room and into fresh air and noise, and they continued to wait for the report.

Over an hour later, after the doctor had told them that all had gone well, and after Alene had been wheeled to the waiting room, ready to leave, my father walked back into the hospital and showed them the new watch he had just purchased in a downtown jewelry store. His other watch, itself fairly new and in perfectly good condition, was in his pocket, with his penknife and his exact allotment of coinage; at least two more were at home in his jewelry case.

That seemed to be the start of it, and it had gotten worse in stages. Little things, simple actions, that he had done by rote countless times began to confuse him. He started approaching each task, whether it be eating a sandwich or going to the bathroom or opening the newspaper to read it, as if it were a procedure new to him that must be mastered slowly. The book that I consulted during the faculty meeting reported that many people with Alzheimer's lost their tempers easily, or shouted obscenities. None of that happened with my father. He eased himself into his new existence with grace, seeming almost, at times, to not want to get in anyone's way while doing it.

The sun was coming up, through the thick branches of the big trees that I could see from my new study. Sunrises sometimes reminded me of that lake house on Stanmire, and of the ones that I had watched there, from its screened-in porch. My mother and I were always the first ones up, and, when we were at the lake, we made it our business to not miss too many sunrises. Then we would rummage around in the little kitchen, to make coffee and breakfast in pans and pots too dented and stained for use at home, their white enamel outsides nicked, showing bits of black metal, like bad spots on apples.

That was before Mother was sick, of course, when things like pretty sunrises still mattered to her. This one, visible from where I was sitting, was good enough to make me think, for a moment, that I saw Spanish moss in the trees; I could nearly smell the rich, moist presence of the still lake.

Once, when I had been a very small child, Uncle Gaston and Aunt Billie and some more of the Rozelles came down to the lake house. One old man, who was the husband of some cousin of my father's, came with them. He didn't look directly at people when they looked at him, and usually didn't answer questions when they were asked. His wife had to hold on to him when he shuffled along, and he smiled to excess, in my young opinion. He was, I suppose, the first old and confused person that I had ever been thrown into contact with, and I watched him like a hawk during his stay. On the second afternoon, he got up from his nap and wandered around to the side of the house, where the fishing poles and tackle were kept. I went off to do something else, and, when I got back, I saw him down on his knees. I thought, for a moment, that he might be praying, or maybe looking for something he had dropped. Then he raised one of his wrinkled hands to his head, and I could hear his faint crying, like a puppy might do outside a window. I told my father, and he and Uncle Gaston went to him, removed the fishhook that he had caught in his forehead, and helped him into the house, where several of the women tended to his wound and put him to bed. The old man had mumbled a good bit, and maybe cried a little, and was still mumbling when he drifted off to sleep. Uncle Gaston had just nodded his head, and clacked and wheezed. "It's a goddamn shame," he said, clicking the ice in his Old Crow. "He doesn't know where the hell he is anymore."

Later that afternoon, while my father sat beside the grill full of chickens, and my mother sat beside him, looking out at the lake, he made his only comment about the situation. "How can somebody not know where they are," he asked, "if they're *there*?"

He didn't say any more, but it had been obvious that it was on his mind. My mother hadn't answered him, but sat and watched the lake under a perfect sky, into which a couple of slow-moving dark clouds appeared, like harbingers.

f i v e

The radio in Chris Stevens's old Ford is doing its best to send out a Blood, Sweat & Tears tune. But there is a wire loose in there somewhere that Chris has been meaning to see to, so we get it only sporadically. A loud blast of "and when I die . . ." is followed by perfect silence, to be finished several seconds later by ". . . to carry on." If we didn't know the song, it would be harder to keep up, but since we do, we can fill in the quiet places with our own performance. The radio station is out of Dallas, and its signal isn't quite strong enough to reach us static-free even if the Ford's radio were working perfectly. So the parts of the songs that we do hear are emitted in sizzles and pops, like code.

It is almost Christmas, and we are in the throes of a blue norther. Chris had to scrape ice off the Ford's windshield before he came to get me, and the big, white rounded car is sputtering along in the cold night. Every once in a while it nearly stops altogether, like the radio, but then it seems to catch its breath and keep on. The Ford will get us there, I guess; it always gets us there.

The steering wheel is as big as one you would expect to see in a bus or a big rig truck. Chris leans on it when he drives, and taps his fingers in time with the music. We both keep an eye on the dark sky for any evidence of snow, but so far there hasn't been any. The last time it snowed in Oakwood, other than a few pathetic attempts, was during Christmas seven or eight years ago. Chris and I are seniors in high school.

The stars, usually abundant this time of year, are hidden behind dark, low clouds that don't seem disposed to deliver any snow. They seem capable only of spitting out a miserable mixture of sleet and rain. The ditches beside the dirt road we are traveling on are frozen over, but we haven't done any slipping or sliding to speak of. Most Saturday nights, we'd be on the highway to Buffalo to pick up the two girls that we've struck up an acquaintance with of late. But they've gone off to one of their grandparents for a Christmas get-together, so Buffalo isn't on our agenda tonight.

Tonight we intend to buy a couple of six-packs of beer from one of the local bootleggers, and then drive around for long enough to drink them. Chris and I have already seen the movie playing at the Texas Theater in Palestine, so we figure this night, as dreary and cold as it might be, is perfect for that. Maybe there will be other kids out doing the same thing, and we might hook up with them. But Chris and I are pretty happy with each other's company, so, if the beer is cold—which it certainly should be on a night like this—and at least parts of the songs make it out of the radio, the evening won't be a complete waste.

Icicles have formed on the limbs of trees beside the dirt road, and the edges of the Ford's windshield are glazed over. The radio antenna is coated with ice. I point to it.

"I hope that won't make the station come in any worse than it already is," I say.

Chris looks at it, and taps the big steering wheel. "It'll make it come in *better*, I bet," he says.

I don't know what that's all about, but Chris has always been better at science than me, so there may be something to it. That's the way it's been since we were in elementary school; he has the edge in science and math, and I do best in social studies and English. But our grades in high school wouldn't indicate that either of us is a wizard at any of it.

The bootlegger that we do our occasional business with is an old black woman who lives in a frame house at the top of a hill. The long dirt road that leads up to it is bordered by bar ditches into which we've tossed our precious, ill-gotten cargo more than once, when we saw a set of headlights at the bottom of the hill that looked curiously official. The ditches are iced over tonight, and the old car is making a slow and careful progress up the hill. It's beginning to slip a little on the icy patches in the road, and it feels like a particularly awkward and heavy boat rocking around.

We see several old pickups parked by the small porch at the top. None of them looks like anything that a constable or a county deputy would drive, so Chris turns off the motor, and we step out into the freezing night. Pellets of sleet sting our faces like needles; Chris says a word that a Baptist preacher's son shouldn't say, and I say one that a schoolteacher's son shouldn't. On the porch, we knock loud, hoping somebody will come soon.

The door opens less than an inch, and in the bright light of the room, we can see an old black man squinting at us. He looks us up and down, then pushes the door open just enough to see whether we are alone.

"You boys wantin' some beer, I guess," he says. We nod that we do, slapping our hands together to try to shock some warmth into them.

"Who is it?" the old woman calls from the kitchen, and when she learns that it is two boys wanting some beer, she moves the old man out of the way and pushes the door open, sweeping us into the bright light of the room and the warmth from the heater. The old woman is in a faded print dress, and is barefooted. Three black men, of about the same age as the old woman, are playing dominoes at a table by the heater. They look at us when we enter, and the one whom we know to be the old woman's husband gives a little wave of recognition.

The old woman dips snuff, and is enjoying a large quantity of it now. It causes her lower lip to protrude to what appears to be an uncomfortable contortion, and the black granules of tobacco are evident between her teeth. She pats us on the back, and tells us how happy she is to see us, not unlike the way she would greet someone calling on her from the church. Rumor has it that she is quite a leader in her church and that her husband is a deacon. She asks about our families, and when we inquire reports that she is doing fine. Now she asks how many six-packs we'll be needing for this cold night, and we tell her one each.

The old woman charges three dollars for a six-pack of the lowest-priced off-brand beer that she can find on sale in Palestine. We don't have much choice but to buy it from her, or from one of her competitors, if we intend to do any beer drinking. No alcohol is sold legally in Leon County, and, even if it was, no one would sell it to teenagers. We could drive over to Palestine, I guess, and maybe somebody would sell it to us. But it's a forty-mile round trip, and that's asking a lot of the old Ford for a few cans of beer that we can drive up this hill to get.

I don't think the black kids that go to Oakwood High School with us buy their beer from the bootleggers. At least, I've never seen any evidence that they buy it from this one. I don't know what their source is, but they drink on Friday and Saturday nights like we do. We see them riding around, and sometimes we stop and visit, but we haven't progressed far enough yet to ride around in the same car and do our drinking together. The students in the school seem to have accepted integration fairly quickly, and that acceptance is slowly working its way into the town. The oldest of Brown's sons, the one who wanted the flowerpot, is in school with us now. He's never mentioned that day; neither have I. I finally learned his name, but have since forgotten it.

My father isn't the superintendent of the Oakwood school anymore; he accepted that political appointment, and kept it long enough, a little less than a year, to realize that he is not a politician. Now he is a counselor with the county school district, and will start teaching again next year at the prison unit near Palestine, at an age when most teachers retire.

While the old woman is in the back of the house filling our order, we warm our hands over the heater. She never keeps her stock in the refrigerator in the kitchen, and she is always gone a long time before she reappears with a full grocery sack under her arm. Chris and I have conjectured that she must keep it in another refrigerator on a back porch or in a shed. I once said that I found it a little odd that someone who lived in such a little house would have two refrigerators. Chris reminded me that the profit that she had made off of just the two of us would have bought her a pretty good one by now.

The three men are intent on their game and pay us little attention. One of them takes a sip from a small glass at his elbow, and clicks his false teeth as he thinks about which domino would be best to lead. The icy rain and wind is pushing against the window, and the heat from the heater feels good. There are at least four pictures of Martin Luther King on the walls. One of them is framed, and a black ribbon is draped over its top. Dr. King was killed over a year ago, but he hasn't been forgotten in this house. A Christmas tree stands in one corner of the room, its tiny lights blinking on and off like the radio dial in Chris's car. It's about the size of the tree in our house, and just about as ugly. Mother is sick, and the tree and the house haven't received as much of her attention as they used to. My father and I made an attempt at decorating, but we just aren't as good at it as she was.

The men finish the hand, and the winner gloats a little. They turn to look at us, and the old woman's husband nods again, and smiles. Nobody says anything. "It's mighty cold out there," I say, thinking that something needs to be said.

The three old men nod in agreement, and so does Chris. The man who has been sipping from the glass says that it's too cold to be drinking beer on such a night.

"Now, this heah," he says, pointing at the glass with his finger, "is what you oughta drink of a cold night like this." He takes another sip, and grins in satisfaction as he savors it.

The old woman is back with our loot, and we pay her the six dollars. The man who sipped the drink has gone into the kitchen and returns with two small glasses. "Try a little sup of this heah," he says, and he splashes a small amount of clear liquid from a bottle into each glass. Chris and I drink the offering. It is cold, yet warming, and it gets warmer as it goes down further. It is minty, like mouthwash.

We nod our appreciation, and the old man nods, too. "That there is what you be needin' on a night like this," he says. "Not no beer."

The old woman is pushing us toward the door. "You better just stay with the beer, since that what you used to," she says. The small shot of liquid has reached its destination now, and left a warm trail all the way. I feel warmer already.

"How much do you get for a bottle of that?" I ask the old woman. She tells us.

Chris says that he likes the taste of it, but that he will stick with the beer; five dollars for a pint of anything is a little out of his range.

I am still enjoying the warm glow that the small drink is emitting from somewhere deep within me, and the mint taste that is on my lips. I have seven dollars left of my day's wages for working in the meat market of Nubbin Eldridge's grocery store. And, at the moment, I am more than willing to spend five of it on what appears to be a good investment on a cold, wet night.

The old woman goes back to her stores, and returns with a flat pint bottle of the stuff. I look at the label and discover that it is peppermint schnapps.

The frozen yard scrunches under our shoes as we walk back to the car. The rain is just an icy drizzle now, but it is no less cold, and it keeps us moving at a pretty good clip. Inside the cold car, as we bounce down the long hill, the radio signal is flickering in and out. Sleet taps at the windshield. There is more ice in the ruts of the dirt road now, and Chris shifts to a lower gear.

"I guess we ought to have give her back the beer," he says, "and just got that stuff." He points to the bottle in my hand.

"We'll drink the beer, too," I say, rubbing the smooth glass of the bottle between my hands. "This is just to take the chill off." I turn the top to break the seal, and offer Chris the first sip. He shakes his head.

"I didn't like it all that much," he says. "Too sweet."

This presents a problem of sorts. Whatever we buy from the old woman, we have to drink or throw away since it wouldn't be wise to hide cans of beer around the house. I look at the pint bottle. Then I take a bigger drink than the one given me by the old man. The schnapps burns all the way down. I squint my eyes, and suck in some of the cold air.

"That's the ticket," I say, screwing the top back on. "Like a little fire in your furnace." I offer Chris a drink, and he again declines. He drinks one of his beers, and, in a minute, I drink one of mine.

Within an hour, much of the beer is gone, and most of the schnapps. Chris hasn't had any of the schnapps, and the warm feeling in my stomach in now a steady glow.

Just outside of town, out past the Church of Christ, there is a place where the road forks. One leads to several little communities out in the country, places like Flo, and Ninevah, and Red Branch. Chris lives out on that road. The other one leads to a couple of big ranches, and to the turnoff that goes to Stanmire Lake, where our lake house is located. Both roads eventually run into the highway that links Centerville to Crockett. The spot where the two roads branch away from each other is called the "Y." In most towns and cities that would mean the YMCA, but in Oakwood it means the small triangle between the two roads where people can turn around, or stop and visit for a while.

Chris and I sat here, not too many weeks ago, and pondered our futures. It's an appropriate place to do that, I guess, with roads going off in several directions. It was a nice afternoon in late fall, and the last of the geese were drifting over us on their way south. We sat in the Ford and talked about going off to college, or jobs, and on to the rest of our lives, whatever they would be. The geese had a better idea where they were going than we did, and we didn't reach any conclusions. We hardly ever do.

The "Y" is our communications center on Friday and Saturday nights. There is almost always somebody parked there, waiting for someone else to show up. Sometimes, there are seven or eight cars or pickups there, all with the windows down, everybody sipping their beer and calling out to each other. Tonight there is a single car, and its windows are closed tight against the winter weather.

Chris recognizes the car, and tells me who it belongs to; he is seeing better than I am at the moment. We pull up beside it and, in a second, the occupants of that car are in the back seat of this one, cursing the cold night and the rain and sleet. It is two boys a couple of years younger than us, and one of them is talking so fast that the window beside his face is steaming up from all the activity. He is telling about a couple of girls from Palestine who promised to meet them tonight and failed to show. They had met at a church Christmas party and the girls had promised and all, but the two boys have been driving around for two hours, and haven't seen a sign of the girls. The other boy calls the missing girls a couple of names that he probably didn't learn at that church Christmas party. The fast-talking boy slows down for long enough to listen to his companion's assessment, and to agree with it. They ask if we have any beer.

"Why don't you go buy your own beer?" Chris asks.

The fast-talking boy says that they had assumed that the two girls would bring the beer, since they were home from college for the holidays and wouldn't have any trouble buying beer at a store.

Chris turns in the front seat of the Ford and stares at them for a long time before he speaks.

"Why in the hell do you think that two college girls would drive all the way from Palestine to Oakwood just to ride around in an ice storm with the two of you?"

They don't answer. Chris continues to stare at them. "Are you crazy?" he asks. The boys don't have an answer for that, either. They ask again if we have any beer. We give them a couple.

After we've all finished a beer, I take out my pint of peppermint schnapps and hold it up to see how much is left. Chris turns on the interior light so that I can see; the bottle is half empty.

"What is that?" the fast-talking boy asks, when the light is off again. The radio is in one of its silent intervals, and the only sound is the slight scraping of sleet as it pelts against the windows.

"Fire," I answer. "Fire for the furnace."

The two boys accept the answer, and say they wouldn't mind a sip of it. I pass the bottle back to them, and, in a minute, the sound of two loud intakes of breath comes from the dark back seat.

"That's what you need on a cold night like this," I tell them. "Not beer." Chris looks at the beer that I am in the process of drinking.

The fast-talking boy hands the bottle back up to me, and I take a liberal swig. I can't taste the sweetness of it anymore, but the fire is still there. I search for something important to say, but nothing comes to mind, so I take another drink.

"You better go easy on that stuff," Chris says. "You been drinking beer, too."

I tap the window with my finger, to call his attention to the dreary night out there. "Got to stoke the furnace," I tell him.

Soon, my furnace is stoked sufficiently to take on any blizzard thrown my way. Chris seems to be arguing with the boys about my needing to go on home, and they maintain that what we all need to do is find the girls from Palestine who might, after all, have been detained, or may be lost and trying to locate them. Chris says something about anybody who would get lost in Oakwood not being worth the effort. I can barely hear them.

Some time passes, and Chris is gone. I am in the back seat of a different car and the two boys are in the front seat. The fast-talking boy is on the passenger side; he's louder than the radio, which seems to work better in this car than the one in Chris's Ford. We are moving, and the icy rain is still coming down. I guess we're looking for the girls from Palestine.

We drive by the Methodist church. They don't put the plywood Nativity scene up anymore, since too many seasons in weather such as this finally took their toll. The shepherds and kings were notched and faded. Even a chunk of the baby Jesus had come off. I look at the empty place beside the church where the scene used to be every year. Mother and I would come down here just to look at it. We wouldn't come now, even if it were brand-new; I doubt that we could sit in a car together without arguing. The smallest of things sets us off, and all of our time together now seems to be spent snapping and biting at each other. My father says that I'm just mad at her for being sick, and that she is mad at herself for the same reason. I'm beginning to think that we just don't much like each other anymore.

The two boys in the front seat have finally reached the inevitable conclusion that the two girls are still in Palestine. One of the boys calls the girls bitches, and the other one says they're whores. I watch the rain, with small bits of ice in it, move in little rivers across the surface of the window beside me. I tilt the bottle of peppermint schnapps and drink the last of it. The oily residue left in the bottle slides down the glass like the rain on the car's window. In a minute they become the same thing.

Now the two boys are gone, and I am sitting on the porch swing by our front door. There is the stack of wood that my father keeps out here for handy access. I point to it, in recognition. The winter rain is peppering down on the roof of the porch, and I hear the pellets of sleet falling on the concrete steps. Annie Bell used to sit out here and watch me when I played in the yard, telling me constantly not to go over by the "ruet," her word for road. The highway that she was so concerned about is slick tonight, and not too much bothered by traffic. After a few minutes a big truck flies by, throwing up water and mist behind it, and then it is quiet. I think of all of our dogs who were killed on the highway, and of Bo, who almost was, and who has long since gone on to join them anyway.

It's obviously cold out here. After all, it's sleeting. But I'm not cold. I guess I have enough schnapps in me to serve as antifreeze. The swing feels good, but I know better than to rock right now. Still is best. I wonder if the boys found the girls from Palestine, or if they just went on home after depositing me.

There aren't any lights on in the house across the highway, or up the hill, in Miss Mae's house. It must be late.

The narrow slats of the swing are smooth under my hand. My mother used to sit here and read her new cookbooks that came from her book club. My father would collect the mail, ours and the school's, about midmorning every day, and, if one of Mother's cookbooks came, he would drive it out here in the school car so she could have it sooner.

I'll bet she hasn't read a cookbook in years. Or sat on this swing either.

That's daylight coming in my window, and I'm in my bed. I close my eyes and try to get some kind of dead reckoning as to the situation beyond these two simple facts. I can smell coffee from the kitchen, and bacon. The coffee smells good; the bacon doesn't.

The first thing needing doing is the brushing of teeth. I don't know if there's enough mouthwash in the bathroom cabinet, or in the whole town, to negate the foul stench that currently resides in me. Covers are thrown back, and a little wobbling is needed to achieve enough balance to avoid falling back into the bed. All is numb, except for the head. Aspirin tablets will be needed after the mouthwash.

My clothes are folded neatly and draped over the chair, the socks perfectly parallel over the blue jeans. My loafers, much in need of cleaning after sloshing through ice and mud, sit side by side on the wooden floor.

A shower clears the head somewhat, and the aspirin may be kicking in. While dressing, possibilities present themselves. Options.

The flu has been going around. Maybe a particularly severe and sudden occurrence will be credible. Not likely, is my guess. Maybe I brought myself in and put myself to bed. The uniform on the chair belies this one. These are hopes, nearly prayers; there is only one reality. The man I hear shuffling slowly around in the kitchen, cooking breakfast, performed the cold, middle-of-the-night duty of putting a drunken son to bed. And he is as embarrassed, and as reluctant to see me, this morning, as I am to see him. A cheerful, nothing-wrong-here entry won't work, neither will the hangdog, gee-I-messed-up-this-time approach. My father deals with facts, and doesn't like them smoothed over or altered.

Mother is sitting at the kitchen table, smoking a cigarette and staring at a mug of coffee. Of course she wouldn't miss this, probably dragged herself out of bed just for it. Her orange housecoat isn't as bright as it used to be. Maybe it's a different one.

My father is frying eggs in the skillet, pushing little waves of grease over them as he's always done. Little waves of grease aren't what I need to focus on at the moment; I sit down at the table. He hasn't looked at me yet.

Mother is looking at me. "You had a late night," she says. When she doesn't get a response, she takes a sip of her coffee. "But then," she goes on, after a moment, "I guess you don't remember much of it."

I want to see my father's face, to get an idea of what he is feeling. But I don't dare look. Not because he would mind me looking, or even know it. But because of what I might see there.

"That's right," I tell my mother. "I don't remember much of it."

Everybody is quiet for a moment. He has lifted the eggs onto plates and stirs the pancake batter once or twice before commencing the last stage of his ritual.

Mother breaks first, and launches into a fast-paced account of the night's proceedings, though I am not sure just how much of them she actually saw. It is unclear to me just which one of them discovered me passed out in the swing on the front porch, but it is patently clear who it was that got me up, undressed, and to bed.

He continues to cook the pancakes.

Mother is quiet now, and drinking her coffee. In previous years she would get up from this table and be about her Christmas chores. The tree would need tending to and looking at; pies and cheese logs would need making. Christmas is gone from her now, and that part of her that was once the brightest part is as vacant as the yard at the Methodist church where the Nativity scene used to be, as removed from her caring as I am.

She is gone, now, back to her bed. We can hear her coughing from their room. The smoke from her cigarette hangs over the table. The accusing and knowing look remains, also, just as dense.

My father puts her plate of eggs and pancakes in the oven, so that she can eat it later. Probably he'll end up throwing it out, since she usually never gets around to eating much of her food anymore.

He puts our plates before us, arranges his knife and fork just the way he wants it, and takes a sip of his coffee. I don't know what to say to him. There don't seem to be any words in my vocabulary big or meaningful enough to convey what I want him to know. So I am quiet.

The thickness in my throat and the hollow emptiness

in my stomach are already in their places, where I know they will be for a while.

"What about punishment?" I finally say. "Do I have to do something extra?" I balance an empty juice glass on its end; the last of Mother's cigarette smoke is fading away. "Or not do something?" Payment seems due.

He looks at me for the first time.

"How do you feel right now?" he asks.

It's an effort to get the words out; my eyes are still on the juice glass that I am balancing. "Worse than I've ever felt in my life," I tell him.

It is as completely quiet as a room can be now. I lift my eyes to meet his. He looks at me for a short moment, and then turns his attention to his breakfast.

s i x

September 1991   The new school year had barely started when Alene called to report that my father had fallen in the yard while she was at the grocery store. He had been taking one of his many naps when she left, and when he woke up had probably gone into the front yard to make sure that their American flag was secure in its holder, a pilgrimage he made several times daily. The neighbor who spotted him, lying still on the lawn, said that he either couldn't or wouldn't get up. Several other neighbors came to help, and it was this congregation that Alene found in her yard when she returned with her groceries. He was in the hospital in Longview now, with no broken bones and in no danger. But he was, Alene told me, very confused and upset by the whole thing.

He had, she went on to tell me, been more befuddled since his bout with the flu and had become lost in the house several times. She would find him standing in the middle of a room, gazing about as if he had never been there before. She had been worried, of course, and felt it best, after his fall and the subsequent emergency room examination, to have him admitted to the hospital for whatever tests his doctor felt were necessary.

She asked Janie, Diane, and me to come. Decisions, she said, would have to be made. These were the decisions that had been lurking out there, somewhere, in fog and shadow, only possibilities until now.

So here I was again, driving north. I had left lesson plans with the substitute teacher who would keep my classes for two days. It was Thursday; surely whatever problems awaited us could be resolved by Sunday. Janie and I were to meet Diane at five o'clock at the doctor's office where she worked in Tyler, then we would have dinner at a restaurant and drive over to Longview together.

Approaching Houston, I looked at my watch and saw that I would be arriving in Tyler much earlier than I'd planned. So I took the Dallas exit and worked my way onto Interstate 45, which was something of a detour, but it would take me through Oakwood. Two hours later, I left the freeway at Buffalo and drove through the small town and headed north on Highway 79.

Fifteen minutes later, Oakwood lay at the bottom of the hill that I had topped. From up there, it looked the same as it had when I had been a part of it. Seeing it again, sleepy and small and not too bothered by the rest of the world, I knew that it was still part of me.

Climbing out of the car in Miss Mae's driveway, I instinctively looked around for Brown, and almost wondered, since it was not long after lunch ("dinner" in

Oakwood), if I might sit by his upturned bucket and eat his hot water corn bread. But Brown had been dead for years. His had been one of the names that Diane had read in her daily perusal of the "East Texas Deaths" section of the Tyler paper. Nearly every time we talked, she'd inform me of a new addition to the catalog of the Oakwood dead. Every name she mentioned made me feel that a little bit of something was missing, or, maybe, had fallen into place. Particularly when I learned about Brown. Before I had even ventured out into the world beyond our yard and Miss Mae's hill, he had been my first friend.

I walked down to the hedge and looked at our old house. It wanted a coat of paint, but it was still home. The same porch swing was there, and the front yard looked considerably smaller than it had when it had been a fairly big piece of my world. That there was once a gap in the hedge was probably noticeable only to me. I guessed that it had either grown together after Brown died, or perhaps Miss Mae told him to let it grow since we weren't there anymore.

I considered knocking on the front door and asking the people who lived there if I might look around. I would explain to them that I had grown up here and just wanted to walk through the rooms again. Long ago, if someone had presented himself at our door with such a proposition, my mother would have happily served him pie and coffee at the kitchen table. She had loved visitors. Hoboes who came from the railroad tracks across the highway must have considered her an easy mark. Several times a year one would tap on our door and she would bring him a sandwich and something to drink. Janie and I would always tell our father about it, and he would tell Mother that it was a bad idea, but the next hobo that showed up always got fed. Perhaps the hoboes were the first to read the changes in my mother; they quit coming around after she got sick.

I looked at the small, rusted bracket over the front porch, put there long ago to display a flag. I thought of the sad November day of President Kennedy's funeral. Two Roman Catholic nuns had knocked on our door to ask if they might watch the service on television with us. They were from way up north, and had seen the flag mounted over our front porch, which my father had somehow positioned at half-staff on its short pole. I guess they figured that anyone who would go to that much trouble must be watching the funeral. Mother served them lunch, which was no surprise to any of us; anyone who would feed hoboes would almost certainly not turn away nuns. The rituals were strange to a bunch of Methodists and the sisters explained everything for us.

The grown-over gap in the hedge confirmed my decision not to try to visit. The furniture and drapes and pictures, and, of course, the people, would all be different. And I wanted them all to be the same.

There was no answer at Miss Mae's door. Flossie no longer worked there; I had learned on a previous visit that a lady came in twice a week to clean, and that Miss Mae ate most of her meals at the Little Miss Cafe, the only restaurant in town now that Laurene's and the Bus Stop Cafe had long since served up their last chicken-fried steak and hamburger. Her Cadillac was in the garage, but, since her eyesight had deteriorated, her friends or her sister usually drove her wherever she needed to go. She didn't seem to need to go many places anymore. She had once made yearly treks to Las Vegas, and occasionally went to Hawaii, but most of her traveling now seemed to be limited to riding down to the Little Miss or to her daily game of bridge. She was, no doubt, playing now, sipping iced tea and tapping her reading glasses on the table, waiting for the cards to be dealt.

Heading toward town, I turned onto the school road and drove slowly by the new building, dull and modern, that sat where the long, handsome red-brick school had been. The superintendent's office was now in an adjacent structure off to the side. My father wouldn't have liked that, I thought; he wanted his command post in the exact center of the building, so that nothing happened without his knowing it.

Students were milling around outside; it was undoubtedly a class change. A few of them had on blue-and-gold letter jackets, with large O's on the fronts. They talked and laughed and pushed each other, and nobody seemed concerned with the color of anybody else's skin. The groups that I could see were all multicultural. Good for you, I thought. You made it.

There was no reason for me to stop; the hallways and classrooms that I remembered were gone, burned down by a vandal several years before, and no teachers remained from the time when I was a student.

As I was about to turn around at the top of the hill, I turned instead into the town's cemetery, and drove along the curving dirt road to the grave that I hadn't visited in a long time. Finding it, I bent down to brush away some leaves and twigs, and to pull up the weeds that had grown up by the stone. Looking at his name chiseled into the granite, I remembered Jimmy's face, handsome and young and smiling, and his funeral, just six months before the funeral we had watched on television with the nuns. And I remembered my sister Diane sitting in the front row of the Methodist church, widowed and left with three small children, holding Lynn, the baby, in her arms, not taking her eyes off the closed casket in front of her. Jimmy had driven away, one early May morning, to a pipeline job and had probably gone to sleep while driving too fast. He was found in his car at the bottom of a steep gully near Rusk.

I wiped the headstone off with my handkerchief and tried to rout the dirt out of the letters of his name. I stood up and looked down the hill at the school. My father had said that Jimmy was the best football player that ever played for Oakwood. His grave lay not much more than a stone's throw from the field where he had known his brief glory.

Walking around the small cemetery, I found old friends among the stones. Here was Mr. Lancaster Johnson, who owned the grocery store where I bought Dreamsicles from his frost-covered, reach-in freezer. Beside him was his son, Don, who was several years my junior and had died in a car accident. Here was Mr. Deck Moore, the druggist, and his son, Mr. Buck, my father's best friend. The Greer Brothers were here; Mr. Robert, Miss Mae's husband, and Mr. Mack lay close to where Miss Mae would one day be. I thought that it would be appropriate for the Greer Brothers to meet their maker with their ever-present cigars stuffed into the sides of their mouths, but I had seen them both in their caskets, and, unless Miss Mae supplied them at the last minute, they had gone on to Glory without them.

Brown and Annie Bell would not be up here, but in the black burying ground beyond the fence. It occurred to me, as I got back in the car, that I probably knew more people here than I would in the town down the hill.

Driving through the cemetery gates, I felt a little sad that my father would not end up on this hill, among his friends and neighbors. But his name was already chiseled into a stone in the little Shiloah Cemetery, near where he had grown up. The place that would be his grave one day lay beside another grave which I found it so very hard to visit.

Late that afternoon, as we walked through the parking lot toward the Longview hospital, my sisters and I took a collective deep breath, all of us knowing that a very few steps were taking us from one phase of our lives into another.

I realized that I had been lucky in sisters. People who knew us often commented on how close we were, and how happy we all seemed when together, especially if they remembered Janie and me when we were young and how badly we got on then. Ours was a relationship built solidly on mutual respect and love. We managed to do what so many families fail at: we enjoyed each other. And now we had a hard thing to do, and I could feel their tension next to me as I walked.

"Let's just see what the doctor has to say," I said as we stepped through the automatic doors of the hospital. "Maybe it's something they can treat with medication." Janie and Diane nodded that this might be so, but we all knew that it probably wasn't.

Alene met us at the door of his room and began crying, hugging each of us in turn. She was a crier and hugger of the highest order.

"I just didn't know what else to do, honey," she sobbed. She called everybody honey, so it was unclear which of us she was speaking to. Alene looked awfully tired, having stayed at the hospital the last two days and nights, trying to sleep on one of those contraptions the nurses referred to optimistically as a "sleep chair." "It's been so hard." She blew her nose into a tissue. "I just don't know if I can look after him anymore." So we came quickly to the point of this visit.

We all assured her that she had done the right thing.

"And he's so sweet," she continued. "He never complains."

My sisters nodded in agreement, and tiny star-points of moisture appeared at the corners of their eyes. I felt that I had better move things along.

"What does the doctor say?" I asked.

"They ran lots of tests." Alene wiped her eyes and took my hand. "He's just old. You all know that he's gotten more and more confused all along." She began to sniff and I knew that another onslaught of weeping was on the way. "He gets lost in the house," she managed to say, between sobs, "and I can't get him to understand the simplest things."

"Is it Alzheimer's?" Janie asked.

"The doctor called it something else," Alene said. She thought a moment. "Detra-something."

"Dementia," Diane offered, always the nurse. "Alzheimer's is a form of dementia."

"What does that mean?" I asked.

"He's just old," she said.

In his room, he looked at all of us as we gathered around his bed; Alene took his hands in hers.

"Look who came to see you, Mr. Rozy," she cooed, in her most cheerful voice, as if she were talking to the smallest and slowest of children. I had noticed, through the years, that she talked baby talk more and more around him as he got older, and especially during the last year, when he had started to forget things. He put up with it, and even seemed to enjoy it. If anyone, my mother or anyone else, had talked in such a way to him in his prime, he wouldn't have dignified it with a response, but would have turned and searched for better-behaved people to communicate with.

It bothered me that she talked that way to him, but I kept my mouth shut. When she did it, it was as if part of the pride and dignity that he had always worn, like clothing, was seeping away.

He didn't seem to have heard Alene the first time, so she asked him again if he knew who had come to see him.

"Who?" he asked, clinching his lips into his familiar smile.

She laughed, and cooed some more. "Why, all your babies."

He smiled, but looked somewhat confused, which was understandable, since we were all over forty years old, and I, alone, represented a baby weighing in at well over two hundred pounds and standing over six feet. But he seemed to know us, and smiled to show us that nothing was wrong here, that we'd all go outside to cook chickens and drink Old Crow in a little while. "Good," he said.

Janie and Diane kissed him, and I held on to his hand while we said our hellos.

After a while, we sent Alene home to get some rest and the three of us sat with our father and talked of Oakwood. He had nothing to offer, but seemed to enjoy the conversation. At one point, Janie, who sat on the edge of his bed holding his hand, said, "We're not letting you talk much, are we, Daddy?" He looked at her and smiled. "I just like to listen," he said.

Later, as Diane and I were about to leave, he looked at his wrist, where one of his various watches should be, and asked if it was time to go. We told him that Janie would spend the night with him and that Diane and I were going to sleep at his and Alene's house. He smiled and said, "Good," as he always did, and settled back on his pillow, seeming to understand the plan.

Alene always got up long before the sun and was at his bedside when he woke up the next morning. Janie said that he beamed when he saw her, and held her face in both hands as she kissed him. There was never any doubt of their love for each other, and my father was more affectionate with Alene than I had ever seen him be with our mother. He had been Alene's teacher in the little high school in Alto just after his return from college, and the relationship between the pretty eleventh grader (that was as high as the grades went then in rural schools) and the young teacher and coach had become something more than the usual teacher–student bond. Their romance lasted for a sweet summer at the end of that year and then he moved to Oakwood to teach and coach. They each had married and raised their families and lived the long years in different towns and didn't see each other again until Alene, a widow, wrote to him, asking him to dinner at her home in Longview. And he had gone, and they had come to know each other again. Not too many months had passed (better sooner than later, they figured, at their ages) before I was the best man at their wedding and my father had finally retired from teaching, after a half century in the ranks. He spent his time with Alene playing cards and taking long walks on the winding trail near their house. Theirs had been a good marriage, and two lonely people had found one last dose of happiness.

We spent all of that day at the hospital. When the doctor came on his morning rounds he encouraged us to find a nursing home as soon as possible. He would be better cared for there, the doctor said, and Alene, not up to tending to him all the time, could visit him every day. We knew this, of course, but having the doctor say the words to us made the decision easier. Janie, Diane, and Alene visited three places that afternoon, while he and I watched a baseball game on the television in his hospital room. At least I watched it; he watched me. They chose a nice place called the Clairmont, spacious and clean and friendly, and arranged for him to be admitted the next day.

I stayed with him that night in the hospital, and spent much of it standing at the side of his bed, watching him sleep. The hospital's intercom system dinged away through the night, and the nurse checked in from time to time.

So we've come to this, I thought, watching his wisps of white hair rise and fall with each soft snore. And we're putting you where you never wanted to go, and where I don't want to put you. He had once told me, even before he married Alene, that when he got very old he would like to live in the Methodist retirement home in Galveston. It was in the old Buccaneer Hotel on the seawall, where we used to stay on our annual trips to the beach. But he had envisioned a room with a kitchenette, where he could make his own meals and read the paper and watch television and take walks beside the Gulf of Mexico. He had been in good health all of his life, had taught school for fifty years, had fought in a world war, survived a depression, raised his family, and buried his dead. He had never had a reason to suspect any of this.

And yet he had feared it. We had seen his fear as he had watched his older sister change from a witty, intelligent person into a bewildered old lady, unsure of where she was or where she had been. He had worried about her, and, almost certainly, about himself. As he began to forget more and more simple things, he must have wondered how far behind her he was.

Late in the night, as I was half dozing in the horrible sleep chair, I heard the covers rustling on his bed. He watched me stand up, and I could tell that he wondered what I was doing there, or, maybe, what *he* was doing there.

"Did you get some sleep?" I asked him.

He nodded that he had. He yawned and rubbed his fingers through his white hair, then he studied the dimly lit room for a long time. "Where are we?" he finally asked.

"We're in the hospital, Daddy," I told him, leaning on the bed's side rail. "I'm spending the night with you." He nodded that he understood. "Alene and Janie and Diane will be here in the morning."

"When can I go home?" he asked. We had avoided this issue with him for the simple reason that, until now, he hadn't asked.

"We're checking you into a place tomorrow where you can rest and get better."

He stared at me, seeming to know who I was, this time. "How long will I be there?" he asked.

"Until you're well enough to go home," I said, not believing the words as I said them.

He didn't believe them either. He looked out the large window into one of the darkest nights either of us had ever seen.

"Probably for the rest of my life," he said, still looking out the window.

The black Navy surplus clock over the telephone shows five-thirty. It is a heavy clock, with a round glass face which tilts up on a hinge so that it can be wound. My father winds it every morning with the small key he keeps on a nail in a cabinet in the utility room beside the kitchen. The clock is mounted to the end of the cabinet with heavy screws and can be seen from the table in the kitchen. I learned to tell time on that clock before I ever went to school, and Miss Francis, my first-grade teacher, had a difficult time making me understand that it was half past one, not thirteen-thirty.

It is early morning in Oakwood. I am at the kitchen table drinking coffee and watching my father cook our breakfast. Three perfect circles of batter lie on the long griddle. When the pancakes begin to bubble in their centers, he gently turns them over with a spatula. I can't envision him flipping a pancake in the air, the way people sometimes do on television, since that would leave too much to chance. When a thing can be done without risk, and done as well, he will opt to do it. Now he turns his attention to the eggs cooking in the popping bacon grease in the iron skillet. The rashers of bacon, fried to just the right crispness and color, lie in parallel rows on a section of neatly folded paper towels. The two-pronged fork he used to turn the bacon rests in alignment with the paper. The little tableau would make a fine photograph for a food magazine. Or a geometry textbook.

Watching him move through his patient ritual at the stove, I think that he would have made an excellent golfer or fisherman. But he has never gone in for such things; his only hobbies are watching the Dallas Cowboys and the Texas Rangers on television and keeping the yard of our house mowed and clipped. Mother and I are avid readers, but my father, who reads the *Dallas Morning News* and the *Palestine Herald Press* every day, has never, to my knowledge, read a novel. Neither is he very interested in movies, though he sometimes sits with me when I watch one on television. I used to study the program listings in the paper every week to see if there were any Dana Andrews films on; my father went to high school and college with Dana Andrews, and he will watch anything with him in it, more to see his old friend than to follow the story line.

He brings our breakfast to the table and sits down. Silently, we begin to eat. It is a cold January morning, but there is no fire in the fireplace in the living room since we will be leaving soon. It's still dark outside, and the panes of the kitchen windows are frosted over with the cold.

"You're all packed, I guess?" he says, slicing his pancakes into equal pieces. He knows that I am; my duffel bag has been by the back door since last night.

"All packed," I tell him, through a mouthful of bacon.

The kitchen is still and lonely, as rooms usually are when departure is imminent, as if they already feel the emptiness to come.

"We'll miss you," he says. "It's been good having you home again." I've been here for a month, on leave between basic training at Fort Ord, California, and my permanent posting in Germany. He will drive me to the airport in Dallas today.

"I've sure had a good time," I manage to say. Words are heavy this morning. I know that it will be quite a while before we will sit down to another of his breakfasts.

"Don't forget to call when you get to Fort Dix," he says. "I'll be home before you get there." I nod.

"How long will you be there, do you think?" he asks.

"They said a couple of days." I slosh the coffee around in my cup. "It's just a processing station for everyone going to Europe."

"Will you go on a military flight or an airliner?"

"Military, I guess."

He takes a sip of his coffee and smiles. "I went all over the South Pacific in the war," he says, "and never set foot on a plane." He still hasn't.

"You went everywhere by ship?"

"Yep," he says, taking a bite of eggs. "Lots of them."

We continue to eat our breakfast in silence.

"I guess they issued you plenty of warm clothes," he says, after a few minutes. "It will be mighty cold in Germany."

"It'll be cold at Fort Dix, too," I say. "The paper says they had heavy snow in New Jersey yesterday."

"Well," he says, moving the last of his pancakes around with his fork, struggling, as I am, to find enough words to keep our conversation going, "stay warm." He looks at my plate. "Are you finished?"

I nod, lifting my plate and taking it to the sink. "I'll sure miss your cooking." He does all the cooking now.

"You go on and see if you forgot anything," he says. "I'll see to the dishes." He squirts some soap into the sink and turns on the hot water. "We need to leave before long; your mother will be expecting us."

Mother is in the hospital in Tyler, one of her frequent trips there for her cancer treatment. We'll stop to see her on the way to Dallas.

The horizon is just beginning to turn pink as we drive through Oakwood. Bobby Stroud's pickup is already parked in front of his hardware store, and one of the grocery stores is open for business. The city limit sign at the edge of town still says "Population: 716," due, I know, to disinterest on the part of the census bureau rather than a coincidental average of births and deaths. The cemetery on the hill is the only thing growing in town.

We don't talk much on the way to Tyler, but watch the gray, cold landscape emerge in the early morning. As we go through Palestine, my father speaks for the first time since we got in the car. "Now, if you forgot anything, I can send it to you."

"I didn't forget anything," I say, looking out the window.

I am in my Class A uniform, my single ribbon—the one that everybody who draws breath gets—in its lonely position over my pocket. I do have a medal, from basic training. I didn't win honors for being proficient at regular shooting or for throwing hand grenades, though I managed to throw them far enough to not blow anybody up. But it turns out that I can shoot with great accuracy from the prone position, so I got a medal for that. I'll be a great asset to the Army in the event that we go to war, provided I can persuade the enemy to give me enough time to lie down on my stomach to get a shot off.

In Tyler, we drive past handsome old houses with yards pretty enough to be parks, like Miss Mae's yard in Oakwood. Tyler is an attractive town, famous for roses and red-brick streets. The brick streets are gradually disappearing, covered over, so as to be not so treacherous on icy mornings, I guess. The town is billed as the rose capital of the world, an assertion that Pasadena, California, would probably find fault with. My sister Diane has lived here for years. After her husband, Jimmy, was killed, she enrolled in the East Texas School of Nursing and, after graduation, went to work as the office nurse of a urologist; she's been there ever since.

Mother is sitting up in her bed in the hospital when

we enter her room. Brightly colored pajamas and too much makeup do little to disguise her frail condition. What little hair she has left after her radiation treatments is covered by a neatly wrapped orange scarf. She smiles when she sees us, and presses her thin face to mine as I kiss her. "You look handsome in your uniform," she tells me.

"I fed him a good breakfast," my father says, lowering himself into a chair. "He'll have to make do on Army rations now."

"I hope they feed you good," Mother says, holding my hand. Her pretty eyes, deep in the dark hollows of her face, never leave me, as if they want to drink me in whole before I go. This Army business has brought on a change in the way we deal with each other, as if we are straggling out now, at the end of our bitterness and sniping. It's like we've finally reached a door, and the fresh air feels good. But doors lead to other places, and this one promises to be a sad threshold.

"They say the food's better at permanent posts than at basic," I tell her. I certainly hope so, since it wasn't anything to write home about at Ford Ord. But after all the torturous training the drill sergeants put us through, I ate it readily enough, and even did tricks for it. They had a rule; recruits had to pull themselves along a long section of a raised, horizontal ladder before they could eat the evening meal. I failed at it on the first night, and went to my bunk without my supper. By the second night, I was determined to do it, and I did. I think I would have done a high-wire act, if they had required it, rather than miss another meal.

"I'll send you cakes when I get better," Mother says. I can't remember when she's made a cake.

"That'll be nice," I tell her.

"Lester," she says to my father, "Diane said to call her when you got here. She wants to come over for a minute." The doctor's office where she works is around the corner from the hospital. He dials the number.

Mother goes into one of her coughing spells, and the pain it gives her is evident on her face. When it passes, she blows her nose into a tissue. "Now, don't you worry about us," she says, taking my hand again. "Your daddy and I will be fine." She tries hard to give me a reassuring smile.

"I'll write you lots of letters," I say. Unspoken words hang heavy in the air, like teetering bricks that need to fall. But I can't seem to find them, and the words I say are inadequate and meaningless. "It will probably be too expensive to call."

My father has finished talking to Diane. "You call us collect every once in a while," he says.

"I'll find out how much it costs," I tell him.

He looks at me, then at Mother. "It won't matter."

In a few minutes, Diane arrives, sweeping into the room as she sweeps into every room, seeming to suck up all the air in her wake, drawing everyone's attention to her, making us glad that she's here.

After a little while, my father looks at his watch and

says it's time to go. Diane says that she'll walk down to the car with us, and I wait until they have both told Mother goodbye and gone into the hall before taking the little hands in mine. I know that this may be our last time to see each other; I won't be eligible for my next leave for a year, and her condition, though stabilized, can take a turn for the worse at any time. There is a good-sized lump in my throat that makes it difficult to speak. I hold on to her hands; they feel like the thin bodies of frail birds. These can't possibly be the same hands that decorated all those Christmas trees, and made all of those exotic dishes, and lightly brushed my close-cropped hair when we would sit on the porch swing and I would read to her, showing off my newly learned skill.

"When I get home," I tell her, "I'll expect to see you up and around and making me good things to eat."

"I will," she says. There are tears in her eyes, running down her thin face, leaving a trail through the thick makeup.

"I'll think about you all the time," she says. "And I'll write to you." I can already see those letters, almost impossible to read, in her tiny hen scratch wandering never very close to the lines on the paper. I kiss her, and tell her to get well soon. I hold my face close to hers for a moment and can feel her crying. At the door, afraid to attempt saying anything more, I wave to her. She makes an effort to smile. There are a million things we need to say to each other right now.

My tears don't come in the hallway, or in the parking

lot as I say goodbye to my sister, or even in the car as my father drives us through Tyler toward the Dallas highway. But then they come with a fury, and I bury my face in the handkerchief that he hands to me. I'm embarrassed to be crying in front of him.

"It's O.K.," he finally says, not taking his hands off the wheel or his eyes off the road. "My mama was real sick while I was in the war. When I'd get letters from her, I'd have to go off by myself in the jungle to read them." We both know that she hadn't been there when he got home. He touches my arm. "There's no reason to be ashamed of crying for your mother."

I want to tell him that I know that I've done badly by them. My brief academic career was less than distinguished; I piddled away high school, making just the marks needed to pass. In a class of fourteen, I managed to graduate in the bottom half. I registered at Sam Houston State University because my father and Thomas, Janie's husband, had gone there. After six weeks of skipping too many classes and completing too few assignments, I quit, a decision mutually acceptable to me and the university, and moved home to Oakwood. I found a job at Gibson's Discount Center in Palestine, stocking shelves and selling sporting goods. My father mentioned college often, assuming, I suppose, that I would eventually go there. Mother, who always hoped that I would study to become a commercial artist or a cartoonist, never mentioned it again. I saw the disappointment in her eyes when I left each morning for my job, and I sensed her deep resentment that I had thrown away my talents to sell fishing lures and shotgun shells.

After a year of this, I struck up a friendship with the young student preacher assigned to the Methodist church in Oakwood. He was just home from the war in Vietnam, and was enrolled at Lon Morris College in Jacksonville. He encouraged me, probably at my father's request, to go there with him. So I switched to the evening shift at work and drove to Jacksonville with Tom every day. I passed all my classes and transferred to Sam Houston for the summer term. My father was happy, but didn't seem surprised, as if he had known all along that I would come around. But Mother, in and out of the hospital for her treatments, never asked about my classes or showed much interest in my progress, as if she were waiting for the other shoe to drop. I think I was on probation with her. Once, in one of her dark moods brought on by her illness, or, maybe, her medication, she said that I could always get my Gibson's job back when I failed.

Last summer, I was drafted. Since the war is in its political death throes, I'm being sent to Germany. My plan is to return to Sam Houston after my hitch. My father assumes that I will. Mother hasn't voiced an opinion one way or the other; I suppose that jury is still out.

He is quiet, and keeps his eyes on the highway. I want to tell him that I hope that Mother knows that I am on the right road now, to wherever it is that I'm going. I want to tell him that I realize that all the hurtful things she ever said to me came from her sickness and her pain, and not from her heart. I want to tell him that all the stupid things I ever said to her, to hurt her, came from my immaturity and wounded pride, and not from me. He said once that Mother and I just knew how to rattle each other's cage. I want to tell him that I know, now, that I was mad at Mother for years, for being sick, and for not being the person whom I had loved in my childhood, and whom I missed. I want to tell him these things. But I don't. I sit quiet as a tomb in the car and, soon, the Dallas skyline appears on the horizon in front of us.

Janie and Thomas and their children are at Love Field when we get there; they live not too far away. We eat lunch at a snack bar, then go to the boarding area. Jeff and Lesli, Janie's kids, run to the large window and inspect the plane, connected to the terminal by a covered walkway. After much small talk, stilted and awkward, my flight is called. I hug Janie and the kids, and shake Thomas's hand.

Now I turn to the hardest chore, the one I've been dreading all morning. He shakes my hand and holds it tight. "Don't forget to call when you get there," he says. I've never seen him cry, but I can tell that he's not very far away from it.

"I won't forget," I tell him.

He is still holding my hand. "You just take real good care of yourself," he says. I know that I should say something to him now, but the only words that seem appropriate are Dorothy's to the Scarecrow just before she left Oz. I should tell him that I'll miss him most of all. But I don't. I should tell him that I love him. But I don't. It's been a long day, full of thousands of words that never got said.

"Write to me," I manage to get out, before going through the door to the walkway.

After a few minutes, the plane backs away from its gate and turns slowly toward the runway. My family becomes smaller and smaller at the big window, and then I can't see them at all. Later, I look out my window at the narrow ribbons of highways running over the gray winter landscape, like veins. My father is on just such a highway, I think, on his way home to Oakwood, and to an empty house. He will fix himself some supper and watch a little television before settling down to the newspapers he hasn't read today. And he will wait for my call.

Outside the Philadelphia airport, I find the van full of soldiers on their way to Fort Dix. I show my orders to the driver and take a seat. Snow is falling, the first of any significance that I've seen since that Christmas in Oakwood long ago. The driver points out Veterans Stadium as we pass it.

When we arrive, we're given supper and assigned bunks in large, old-fashioned two-story barracks. After stowing my duffel bag in a locker, I have to report to the processing center to check in. It's nearly ten in Oakwood. Finding a pay phone, I give the operator the number that I know by heart. The snow is coming down faster now, falling silently on the dirty glass of the phone booth. My father's voice accepts the collect call from the operator;

just hearing him speak to her causes the lump to return in my throat. I must have been born with that lump. It must be stored away, just close enough to materialize when needed.

"I'm here," I manage to say.

"Any trouble?" he asks.

I can see him, standing at the phone, under the Navy clock in the hallway between the utility room and the kitchen. It is dark in Oakwood. It was dark this morning when I left, and now it is dark again. The earth has only turned around one time since I was there, where he is now. It seems like it's turned many more times than that.

"Everything went O.K.," I tell him. "I'm on my way to sign in."

He asks if I have eaten. I tell him that I have.

He asks about the weather, and I tell him about the cold and the snow.

We are quiet on the line for a moment. "Do you know when you'll be shipping out?" he asks. I tell him I won't know till I sign in.

"Well," he says, "you call me tomorrow night and let me know the plan. Don't worry about how much it costs." This is considerate license from a man who will drive from one Palestine supermarket across town to another one to save a few pennies on a jar of jelly.

"Call me at work, if you need to." He teaches half days now, at the state prison near Palestine. He asks if I have the number. It is quiet in the cold phone booth; the only sound is the soft flutter of snow on the glass.

"Daddy," I say, swallowing to get past the lump, "I just want to . . ." I don't know how to finish.

Neither of us says anything for a moment.

"I know," he finally says.

"I'll call you tomorrow," I say, and hang up.

Walking toward the processing center, I imagine him lowering the receiver into its cradle and then getting ready for bed. It will be lonely there, with both Mother and me gone, when he turns off the lamp beside his bed.

The processing center is bright and hot and full of soldiers of all ranks sitting on hard chairs, waiting their turns at the many desks where they will be checked in. I find an empty chair between two enlisted men, one a staff sergeant whose bored expression says that he has done this many times before, and one a boy of about twenty, like me, with a single stripe on the sleeve of his uniform. The young soldier and I clutch our orders in nervous hands, as if afraid that someone will try to steal them. The orders are our security, our umbilical cords to a system so complex and mammoth that we would be lost forever without them. We watch the slow process taking place at the desks. "We may be here all night," I say.

The young soldier smiles nervously. "I'm tired," he says.

I tell him I am, too. "Where are you from?"

He tells me the name of a small town in East Texas. He seems pleased just to have the opportunity to say the name out loud.

"Why, that's close to Tyler," I say. "I went through Tyler today." He smiles. "I'm from Oakwood." He nods that yes, he knows where Oakwood is. I ask him if he was on my flight, which I know is unlikely, since I didn't see him in the van earlier. He says that he arrived early this afternoon.

We pass the time talking of East Texas things. The staff sergeant ignores us, and smokes many cigarettes. In a while, he is called to one of the desks.

The young soldier looks at me. "Are you homesick?" he asks. I can tell that he is.

I nod that I am, and we both smile. Our lives have never touched, prior to this night, and will almost certainly never touch again. But there is a kinship now, between us, born of a common geography and of a common longing. It is almost tangible.

Eventually, he is called to one of the desks. Holding tight to his orders, he says, "Be seein' ya," and walks away.

I sit on the hard chair in the brightly lit, hot room and am aware of the bustle of activity as it moves around me and bumps against me. I am not looking at the activity, but at the cold, dark night beyond the windows, and at the falling snow.

Mother is probably still awake in her hospital room, coughing up the residue of so many years of so many cigarettes. She sleeps in sporadic, short stints now, like a cat. She is probably clicking the remote control by her bed, churning the television set through its channels, not watching any of them.

My father is asleep by now, in the back of the house that I can see so clearly, so very far away.

e i g h t

October 1992   A year passed. And we all went, when we could, to visit my father in his comfortable room in the Clairmont. Alene went twice each day, to take him his *Dallas Morning News* in the early morning and to sit with him and watch the birds come to the feeder outside his window each late afternoon. More and more, he didn't try to read the newspaper, but seemed content to just hold it, much as he would gaze in the direction of the small television set in his room but not watch it. He was only half with us now. The rest of that good, crisp mind had found an easier place to be. The only object in the room which held his complete attention for very long was a framed black-and-white photograph of his mother, a stoic-looking country woman with sharp, chiseled features who held my father's heart as he did Janie's. He had been her protector. She had died at the very end of the Second World War, and he, making his way home with millions of other servicemen, had not learned of it until he had arrived. He had had to say his goodbyes to her at her grave, already several weeks old, where she lay beside her long-dead husband in the Shiloah Cemetery, near the little farm where they had raised their large family.

Once, not long after my father and Alene's marriage, I sat on the patio in Longview while he told one of his many stories about his mother. When he had finished, Alene said that he had been his mother's special sweetheart. He thought that over for a long moment. "No," he finally said, "she was mine."

There were other photographs on the walls of his room, of all of us, and one of him in his Army uniform, over which Alene had tacked two small, crisscrossed American flags. But it was the austere picture of his mother which drew his attention most often, and held it the longest.

It hadn't taken him long to become one of the favorites of the nurses and attendants. At mealtimes, he would walk slowly down the long corridor to and from the dining room, using his cane to steady himself, the fingers of his other hand lightly touching the wall, as a small boat might hug the shore on a windy day. He always stopped at the nursing station to visit. They all told us how nice he was to them, and how he always dressed so well. He never left his room, they said, unless he was in clean slacks, shoes with socks, and a knit shirt, the top button always in place. "He's so sweet," one of the attendants told us, whenever she got the chance, "and looks like he's dressed to go visiting." She would always turn at this point, to make sure that no one was listening. "Some of these old folks are mean as sin, and don't care if they got clothes on or not."

Often, on our visits, we would take him to eat at one of his favorite restaurants and, sometimes, to his and Alene's house to sit on the patio. But these trips seemed to confuse him, and he was always ready to go back to his room. Once, on our return to the Clairmont after we had taken him out to dinner, he had seemed especially disoriented. He seemed to think that we were not at our final destination. Standing outside his room, looking around to get his bearings, he asked, "Where do we go from here?" An elderly woman, rolling herself slowly beside us in her wheelchair, stopped and gazed at him, and then at me. "Now there," she said, to no one in particular, "is the question."

The seasons changed, and so did my father. I came away from each visit knowing that he had slipped further back into a time less confusing and threatening. Much of the time, he must have thought he was the superintendent of the Oakwood school again. He would look at the old people in their wheelchairs or moving at a snail's pace in their walkers, and he would say that he didn't know what he was going to do about such teachers. Once, when he was having lunch with Janie in the dining room, he looked at his watch and said that they would have to hurry; he had a class to teach in a few minutes. He always told me he had lots of work to do, and he would look around him, as if to find it.

His roommate was a nice man named Ed. He accepted

Ed's presence, and must have placed him in a category important to his work. Maybe he was the principal. Who knows? The principal of Oakwood High School was never anything more than a figurehead position while my father was superintendent, since he did everything that a principal would have done. When I was in school, I believe Mr. Jacobs and Mr. Snyder took turns being principal. On one of my visits, Ed told me that his foot had been giving him trouble. Looking at it, I saw that it was dark blue, the toes almost black. I asked the nurse at the station about it, and she said that it was a circulation problem, and that Ed's doctor was watching it closely. When I mentioned it to my father, he said that Ed didn't get enough exercise. "He stays at his desk all day," he said.

There came a time when my father couldn't walk down the long hallway to his meals or down to the nursing station to chat. They tried taking him to the dining room in a wheelchair, but he hadn't liked it. Finally, they brought his meals to him so he could eat them in his bed, and his wandering days were over. He still insisted, however, on being dressed in clean, pressed clothes every day.

In September, when he had been at the Clairmont for almost a year, Janie and Thomas and I stayed the weekend at Alene's so that she could visit her sister in Alto. We drove him home on Saturday night and had supper and a visit on the patio. He seemed confused by the surroundings and by us, so we decided, after we had returned him to his room, that it would be best to not take him away anymore.

On Sunday morning, before we started our long drives home, we went to take my father his newspaper and tell him goodbye. He paid more attention to the picture of his mother than he did to us. On the way out, we stopped at the nursing station and Janie asked if our taking him home the night before might be the cause of his doldrums. The nurse, one of his favorites, a large, friendly woman, shook her head and said she didn't think so. "He's just not with us much these days," she said.

Two weeks later, on a Thursday in early October, Janie called in the early morning and told me that he had been taken to the Longview hospital in an ambulance. She was on her way out the door; Diane was going, too. I made quick arrangements at school, and drove to Longview.

It was early afternoon when I pulled into the parking lot; Janie had been watching for me from the window, and met me at the door. "It's bad," she said, taking my hands. I could see that she had been crying. "He had a stroke; they called it massive." She saw the question in my eyes. "They just don't know," she said.

In his hospital room, an antiseptic place, all tile and cold metal, I held his hand and spoke to him. I could tell that he knew who I was, and he gripped my hand with what little strength he could muster. His right side was paralyzed, his face locked into what looked to be a painful contortion. He gasped for air and, though he was on oxygen, I could tell he wasn't getting enough of it. When he tried to talk, he emitted a series of rapid sounds and then frowned, as if to indicate that this wasn't what he had wanted to say at all.

We watched his pain for two days and nights, leaving only long enough to drive the few blocks to Alene's house for a sandwich and a nap. She stayed at the hospital most of the time, hugging all of us and crying a lot.

By Sunday, he had stabilized. The doctor told us that he might stay in this condition for any length of time, and that another stroke, even a small one, would probably kill him. We didn't want to leave him, but we all had jobs to go to. This could last for weeks or months. So we all decided to go home and come back when there was a change.

When I said goodbye to him, I held his hand and told him I loved him. They were words that needed to be said long, long ago. He gripped my hand and closed his eyes, then shot out some of his rapid, codified speech. And then I did something I hadn't done since I was a child; I kissed my father.

I was numb as we all said our goodbyes in the hallway. The sounds and smells of the hospital were all around me as I walked out of the building—doors swooshing open, carts being rolled on squeaky-clean floors, cleanser as thick in the air as it was on the tiles—but I noticed none of it.

Starting the drive home, alone in the car, I prayed that he wouldn't suffer long, and I knew only too well exactly what I was praying for. I knew that life, as he would want to live it, was over. The order and control that had been his daily existence was gone; this new situation was unacceptable, to him and to me. We had never spoken of how he wanted to go, but I knew that this wasn't it, this slow leaking away, like a balloon deflating. I had never known him to give up on anything. I wondered if I wanted him to now.

It started to rain, a slow autumn drizzle at first, then larger, more frequent drops. I turned on the windshield wipers and thought of how he used to let me ride with him, in the school car, when he drove the miles and miles of country roads to make sure that they were safe for the school buses to make their runs on particularly cold winter mornings. Small school districts didn't have transportation directors to do such things; it was one of the duties that fell under the superintendent's wide umbrella. We all would get up a couple of hours earlier than usual on those days, and Mother would fix us a good breakfast, and we'd be off, into the dark, cold morning. We hadn't said much to each other on those trips, but had been happy to just be with each other, watching the lights flicker on in the houses that we passed.

Soon it was raining so hard that I pulled the car over to the side of the highway, to wait for it to let up. Remembering those cold mornings in the school car, I realized that I already was starting to miss him.

I sat there for a long time before I slipped the car into first gear, and started the long, lonely trip home.

n i n e

Miss Mae is gazing through her narrow reading glasses at the cards she has been dealt. The glasses are so precariously perched on the tip of her nose that I expect them to plop, at any moment, into the onion dip. The only thing that prevents this from happening is that they are never left there long enough to fall.

She takes them off, and taps them on the table. "Five," she announces in her loud voice, arranging the cards in her hand.

My father studies his hand as he puffs slowly on his briar pipe. He exchanged cigars for pipes last year; nobody knows why, and, so far, he has offered no explanation. I, for one, am happy with the transition, since pipe smoke is more agreeable than the soot he used to constantly generate. Also, being able to augment a growing collection of pipes has made gift buying, for Christmas and birthdays and Father's Days, an easier chore. A pipe gives him more of a scholarly air than a cigar; it fits him better. In July, he'll have his seventieth birthday, just four days after the nation's two hundredth. He's well into his senior citizenship now, and the pipe suits him nicely. He presses his lips together in concentration as he reaches a decision regarding his cards. "Three," he says.

I am Miss Mae's partner, and, remembering her tendency to overbid, decide to go one shy of what I think I'll make. I bid three. She looks at me over her glasses, which have found their way back to her nose. "Go higher if you want to," she yells across the table. "Mine are solid." She speaks even louder than she used to, if that is possible.

"I know you," I say, checking my hand to make sure all the suits are together. I have a void in diamonds, but haven't bid on it, thinking that Miss Mae will catch some diamond tricks. "I'll just leave a little slack in our rope."

The fourth player is Dison, a teacher at the elementary school, which was the old Dunbar school, before integration. Dison's first name is Barbara, but it is used so seldom that most people have forgotten it. She is divorced, and has two boys in the Oakwood school; driven by boredom, more than likely, she fell into this weekly game. She bids two.

"Somebody's underbidding," my father says, through a haze of pipe smoke. Miss Mae turns her attention back to her cards, and I hope she doesn't change her bid, since underbidding hasn't proven to be one of her tendencies.

We are at the kitchen table in Oakwood, deeply involved in our regular Friday night game of Spades. Dison is emitting steady plumes of cigarette smoke from one end of the table, and lazy curls of pipe smoke drift down from the other end. Miss Mae and I are pretty much caught in the middle.

Miss Mae leads the ace of clubs, which my father, with a smile of satisfaction, promptly trumps. "Pshaw!" she yells—this is as close as she ever comes to an expletive, at least in our presence—and taps her glasses briskly on the table. We end up not making our bid, and she shoots me an accusatory look which says I must do a better job of curbing her excesses.

Soon, the Navy clock over the telephone shows us it is almost midnight. Dison empties her ashtray of its full load, says good night, and leaves. I offer to walk Miss Mae home, as I do every week, and she, as usual, declines. "Anything or anybody who wants to attack an old woman," she states loudly, groping in her purse for her house keys, "can have me." She walks up the hill and through the gap in the hedge to her house. There is only one Greer Brother now; Mr. Robert, Miss Mae's husband, died a few years ago. Old Mr. Mack has probably been sound asleep in his bedroom at the back of the house since before the sun went down. Standing on the back porch, I can hear Miss Mae jangling her house keys as she makes her slow ascent up her hill. Mr. Mack is almost deaf now, and no amount of knocking would bring him to the door. I sometimes wonder if that is why Miss Mae has taken to talking even louder than she always has, in an effort to make him hear her.

My father and I wash out the ashtrays and dishes, put away the cards and score pad, and wipe the table clean.

He asks how my classes went this week; I'm in college at Sam Houston, his alma mater. Nearly every weekend I drive home to Oakwood and the weekly card game. My father is alone in the big house now, and he looks forward to me being there. On Sundays, after accompanying him to the service at the Methodist church, and eating the dinner he cooks for us, I leave for Huntsville.

The GI Bill provides just enough money for me to live in a tiny furnished apartment which I share with another student, Arnie, and his dog, Sugar. Arnie and I are back in school after a couple of years out—he was working in a bank, and I was in the service—and so far we've managed to make it from one paycheck to the next without starving. At the first of each month, we have enough to go on dates and buy an occasional cheeseburger, but, around the fifteenth, our social and culinary lives cease, and we live the remainder of the month on Irish potatoes, which we purchase in large bags, because they're cheaper that way. Arnie and I have become masters at the preparation of potatoes in all of their various possibilities: fried, baked, mashed, boiled, and scalloped. We could write a cookbook.

Arnie is a good roommate. Sugar is another matter. She is a large dog, of indefinite breeding, and not built for a small apartment. She is not a graceful creature, and knocks things over as often as she gets close to them.

Arnie, Sugar, and my Oakwood obligations have done little to enhance romantic pursuits. It is an awkward thing to tell a pretty girl that we can't go to a particular concert or party on a Friday night because I have to drive a hundred miles to play cards with my widower father, his next-door neighbor, and a divorced elementary school teacher. It's almost as difficult as telling her that we can go over to my place, if she doesn't mind being in close proximity to, and probably mauled by, an animal the size of a small horse that runs into things.

When Arnie and Sugar spend the weekend with his parents, my father sometimes comes to Huntsville to visit. He graduated from Sam Houston long ago and commuted there from Oakwood much later, in the 1950s, to take his Master of Education degree. Several of his classmates stayed on at the university as teachers, and now are deans and heads of departments. Some are retired, and a few have died. I've often wondered whether he regrets not staying at the college himself; the dean of the college of education has told me he could have. He has never mentioned it, or wondered, so far as I know, what it would have been like to be a professor or a dean. To him, teaching is a noble and a decent calling, and can be practiced with equal dignity and enterprise in the smallest of public schools as in the largest of universities. I don't know if I chose education as my major because of him. But his influence has been a particularly bright star to steer by.

As we put the finishing touches on our cleanup job in the kitchen, I tell him a little about the material covered in this week's classes. I enjoy my two literature sections the most, and keep him up to date on whatever novels or stories I am reading. He always listens with great interest, but I know that this is foreign ground for him.

"Do you ever read any of the books your mother liked?" he asks. I think about this. She was a fan of Steinbeck, and I recently read *The Grapes of Wrath* for school, but her reading, as voluminous and constant as it was, didn't often include the classics.

"Some," I tell him.

He dries the sink and countertop with a dishtowel, making sure that he doesn't miss any spots. "She sure liked her reading," he says.

The house still seems empty without her. I know it must be especially so for him during the week. She has been gone since January. It is October.

"Did she read as much the last couple of years?" I ask him. I had been in Germany, in the Army.

He gathers up his pipe and pouch of tobacco. "Not so much," he says. "She would read about a new book in the paper, or hear about it on the radio, and I'd get them for her. But I don't think she finished any of them." He pauses, remembering. "They had her on so many different kinds of medicines that I don't think she could keep her mind on it."

He looks at the Navy clock that he winds so carefully each morning. He bought it, before my time, at the military surplus store in Longview where he purchased supplies for the school when he was superintendent. All my life, the clock has been in its place over the phone. Its hour and minute hands are now pointing straight up.

"Are you sleepy?" he asks. He usually goes straight to

bed after the card game. "I'm going to sit on the porch for a bit—if you want to join me?"

It is a cool, autumn night, just before Halloween. The sky over Oakwood is full of stars, and there is a harvest moon. We are on the porch swing, and my father goes through the precise ritual of loading and lighting his pipe. Soon, the only sound is the occasional passing of a car on the highway.

We sit quietly, rocking gently in the swing. It is almost certainly the first time that I've sat out here since he had to collect me, in my peppermint schnapps stupor, and put me to bed.

He pushes a slow train of smoke into the night. "I sit out here pretty regular now."

"It's a nice time of year for it," I say.

He looks at the stars and puffs on his pipe, and a few minutes pass before he speaks again.

He takes a nap every afternoon now, so he stays up later at night than he used to. He watches the beginning of Johnny Carson, till the guests come out, but then he turns it off. He hardly ever recognizes the guests, unless they're really old-timers, so I guess that's when he heads for the porch. He still teaches half days at the prison several miles away, and is home each day by one.

"Your mother and I used to sit on this swing when we bought this house," he says. He is packing the ashes deep into the bowl of his pipe.

"I used to sit out here with her when I was little," I say.

We are quiet again. I know that he is gradually working

up to something, and that he has more on his mind than our family's use of the porch swing. I know, too, that he is weighing words in that fine mind, testing each one before he decides to use it. Finally, he turns and looks at me.

"I guess you're O.K. about your mother," he says. It is a statement, but I can sense a well-disguised question hiding behind it.

"Sure," I say. Knowing this to be not enough of a response, I dig around for something else. The problem is that I don't know what he's getting at. "I miss her," I offer.

He turns his pipe in his hand and studies it from several angles. We rock ever so slightly, as if to remind ourselves that we're on a swing, and are quiet for so long that I think I've provided a sufficiently satisfying response.

"I don't know," he finally says. "It's just that you were away when it all happened." He unzips his tobacco pouch and begins to reload his pipe; I know that he is fortifying himself for the discussion that he is determined to have. Heart-to-heart conversations have never come easy for him; he would rather listen than talk, and he is an absolute master at hiding his emotions. We never had the birds and bees lesson when I was growing up. He pushed that chore off on Diane's second husband, a charming but troubled man who danced through several years of our lives before moving on to bother other people.

"She was mighty sick," he says, lighting his pipe. A single, clear honk from a goose comes through the darkness, then several others join in. They aren't close enough to the orange moon to pick up any of it, and Oakwood doesn't generate enough light to reflect off their white stomachs, so we can't see them. They sing us a few bars of their ancient traveling song, and then are gone. "I know you two had some troubles." He puffs a few times to get the tobacco burning. "You shouldn't think any of it was your fault."

"I should have been here," I say. "I should have come home on leave."

"It was all too quick," he says. "None of us knew what was going to happen." He stops; maybe he's listening for more geese. "Besides, you weren't up for another leave."

"I could have gotten it. They let you take leave before you have it coming."

He thinks about it. "But you didn't know how bad it was," he says.

I had known. I had known there wasn't much time left when I heard her weak, wandering voice on the overseas phone call on Christmas Day. I had known it when I heard his and Janie's and Diane's nervous voices on the same call. I don't tell him this.

"She was so full of all those medicines," he says. "And she was tired of being sick for so long." He doesn't look at me, but looks at the highway. "She was just ready to go."

"She wanted to see me one more time," I say. "She told me so on the phone at Christmas." My sisters have reported that Christmas was a miserable time; they had to open Mother's presents for her, and then she didn't show much interest in them—books that wouldn't get read, other things that wouldn't get used. It was hard for them to watch her suffer through it. My father had made an attempt to decorate the tree and the living room as she had once done, but his efforts had fallen far short of hers. My phone call had ended it; Mother cried, and then went to bed. Soon after that, Janie and Diane gathered up their families and went home.

"It was too quick," he says. "And you were in Germany." He turns to look at me. "There was nothing you could have done if you had been here."

The sound of a train's whistle would be nice now, from either the north or the south, or even a truck zooming by on the highway. But there is nothing, not one single indication that the rest of the world is functioning at all.

"I just wish that it all could have been different, that she could have been happier," I say.

He taps the ashes out of his pipe on the edge of the concrete porch. "She was sick for so long," he says. "She deserved better. She had those problems with her nerves for years, a long time before she got the cancer." He begins to scrape the residue from the bowl of the pipe with his penknife. "And then all those medicines." He obviously blames much on the medicines. He has always been reluctant to take even an aspirin tablet for a headache. "But it wasn't anybody's fault." He stands, having said what he intended to say. "The best thing for us all to do is to remember her when she was happy and well." He opens the screen door to go in. "That's what I do."

Happy and well. Not so much to hope for in life, I think, and usually taken for granted by those lucky souls that are those things. My mother had been happy and well once, but, being the youngest of her children, I had come in at the last of it.

After he has gone to bed, and I am on the way to my bedroom at the front of the house, I stop at the door of the small room that was my mother's refuge during her last year. She said that she was more comfortable in there, and that she worried about keeping my father awake during the night with all her coughing and rustling around. She didn't watch television anymore, and the radio beside her bed was kept tuned, night and day, to a country music station. She had never been a big fan of country music, but the folksy disc jockeys and the simple ballads they played seemed to be a comfort to her. I sometimes wonder if the move to the little room was a logical continuation of her move away from all of us.

It was in that room, on a cold Sunday morning last January, that she lifted the pistol that she had somehow gotten down from the highest shelf of my father's closet and brought an end to her long suffering, of which she figured that she and all of us had had quite enough.

t e n

November 1992   Karen and I drove through Houston at midmorning Saturday among hordes of Christmas shoppers heading for the malls; the girls were home with Karen's father. Eventually, we left the city behind us and headed into the pine trees and pastures that mark the change from coastal to East Texas.

I had not seen my father since the eleventh of October; this was November seventh, almost a month later. It had been an uneasy period in which I had been constantly preoccupied with his condition, his suffering. Not the least of this worry came from a nagging sense of guilt because I couldn't be with him more often. Janie, of course, was wandering through some of the same emotions, and we decided to meet in Longview.

East Texas had, by early November, experienced a couple of heavy jack frosts and at least one solid freeze. The pastures we drove beside were various shades of brown, bordered by pines and cedars interspersed with tall pecans and sycamores straining to shed their few remaining leaves. We stopped between Lufkin and Nacogdoches to eat lunch. The place we chose was on a hill, and a parking lot full of cars and pickup trucks attested to its popularity. The lady who welcomed us explained that the procedure here was to work your way down a long table which held a buffet of fried catfish, hush puppies, fried potatoes, corn relish, and black-eyed peas. Huge cobblers, peach and apple, were on another table. No menus were offered, nor options or variation of any kind, the philosophy of the owner being that anyone who wanted a different sort of food had better just go on down the road to a lesser place. We got in line. And so it was that we arrived, drowsy and full of good country food, for what I was convinced would be my last visit with my father.

He had returned to the Clairmont. I think we all knew that he had been sent back to finish up, to make an end of it. I was glad that he wouldn't die in a hospital; he had never liked them, and had avoided them whenever possible. When my mother had been in and out of so many, he was always on edge, and sat nervously in the lobby, holding a magazine as if he might look at it eventually. The Clairmont was very much like a hospital, but it was also his home, and had been for the last year. This was better. He had lived his life in good places, full of fresh air, and good smells, and sunlight. I didn't want his last moments to be in a cold and lonely place. Here, at least, his things were around him, his television that he never watched, photographs of his family that he sometimes remembered, and sometimes not, and his mother's picture, which he gazed at intently, as if waiting for it to speak. Maybe it would, I thought. Maybe it would be the last thing he sees.

Karen had not seen him since before he had his stroke, and I knew that even though I had described his condition to her she would be shocked. We met Janie in the hall, and one look at her face told me that he was worse. These were looks we had shared before, and they were coming all too often now.

We stepped into the room and said hello to Ed, who was home from the hospital after having had his foot amputated. He looked at the curtain which separated the two beds and back to us, as if to convey, without the burden of words, that things were going downhill here.

I moved around the curtain and saw him before he saw me. What little color he'd had a month ago was gone now. His face was locked into the same contortion, and he was having considerable trouble with phlegm in his throat. The same small sound that had haunted me since I was last with him came from him; almost a question.

Now he saw me. There was absolutely no doubt in my mind that he knew exactly who I was. After a slight hesitation, he closed his eyes and shook his head slowly, letting me know that, between us, there would be no illusions. Our hardest talk, at least in my opinion, had come when I was a junior in high school and had been joyriding, with Chris Stevens, in my father's car. Cathy Johnson, driving to school, had slammed into us. It was my fault; I hadn't been paying attention and failed to yield. I lied to him about it, and told him that a teacher had sent me on an errand before class. He, of course, spoke to the teacher and learned the truth. We had a long visit about truth that night, and I lost driving privileges for what seemed to be a hundred years. He told me that he could forgive me anything, but that I must always, in every circumstance, tell him the truth. We both had pretty much kept our contracts.

And now, on what we both knew was his deathbed, he wasn't going to have any lies. He knew his situation, and he wanted me to know it, too.

I took his hand, dry and frail, and held it next to my face. Karen placed her hand over mine and his and said, "Hello, Lester."

A slight smile came to the half of his mouth that could produce one, and he thrust his lower lip forward a bit before making a sound that might have been "good" or "fine." Then the phlegm erupted into a gurgling cough that came from deep within him. It overtook him completely, and the clinched eyes and pained expression left no doubt as to his opinion of it. Karen went for the nurse.

As soon as she was gone, he settled peacefully back on his pillow, the crisis, for the moment, over. Janie was in the hall, Ed was behind the curtain, and he and I were alone for a minute. He gripped my hand as tightly as he could, and looked at me. The grip and the stare didn't lessen, and I knew that he was trying to tell, or ask, me something.

I looked directly into his one good eye, and held his

hand as tightly as if it were a life rope. The words that I said to him were the only ones that came to mind, the only ones that my voice could make, as if he were drawing them out somehow, with a magnet.

"You can rest now, Daddy. You can get a good rest."

His eye told me he understood. "Everything is O.K. Everything's fine." He seemed to try to grip my hand more firmly, and I moved closer to him. I could smell the foul breath caused by the constant phlegm and drainage; his breathing was wispy and labored. And then, the hardest words of all.

"You can go whenever you want to."

He closed his eye. Our faces were only inches apart now; I tried hard to keep my voice from cracking as I said one last thing.

"We're all O.K."

The final squeeze told me that he understood.

Janie, Karen, and the nurse came in and the nurse swabbed his throat. We stayed a while and, when the time came to go, we all kissed him and held our faces beside his and Janie and Karen told him goodbye. I already had.

Ed read the concern in our faces as we started to leave. He gave us a look which said that it couldn't be much longer now. "Alene and I look after him," he told us. Ed smiled as he looked at his roommate. "Sometimes, when he gets to coughing and carrying on, and trying to talk, I reach over and just hold on to his hand for a little while. And then he calms down." Of the multitude of friends that my father had made in his long lifetime, I thought, this was the last one, as if this special one had been saved until needed.

Just a month before, I had been sure that my father and I had had our last visit. Leaving the Clairmont, with Karen and Janie, I knew that the same gracious power that had sent Ed to him had given us a few more all-important minutes together. Enough time to get a last bit of business cleared up.

eleven

He is asleep on my couch when I get home from work. Since his teaching day is over at noon, and mine lasts till four, he usually gets a good nap in on Friday afternoons. That's when he stops by on his weekly trip to Palestine to buy groceries.

Looking in the refrigerator for the beer with which I intend to celebrate the end of the week, I study the meager purchases that he has temporarily stashed there. It doesn't take much for him, living alone in the big house in Oakwood: a package of bologna, some cheese slices, a quart of milk, eggs and bacon. He eats lunch (he calls it dinner) at the prison every day after his classes are over, and, according to him, he eats well. The prison grows its own crops and raises its own cattle and pigs; in my father's words, it "sets a mighty good table."

I locate my beer and am popping it open when I hear the long, full yawn which announces that he is finished with his nap. He has raised himself to a sitting position, and is putting on his glasses by the time I step into the den.

"Do you have another one of those?" he asks, pointing to my beer. When I've given him one, and he has pulled a lengthy, concentrated swallow from it, he rubs the back of his hand across his mouth and looks at me. "That's good," he says.

I tell him I'm sorry I don't have his brand. He drinks Pearl beer. Once he drank Falstaff, and before that it was Jax. I don't remember him ever drinking more than two or three beers in any given week, but he has always been devoted to his brands of choice. Pearl and Falstaff are hard to find, and I don't believe Jax is brewed anymore; it's as if his slight patronage hasn't been enough to keep their markets alive.

"How was your day?" he asks, slipping his feet into his shoes.

"Fine," I tell him, which is not true. It's been anything but that. It is my first year of teaching and my students have finally reached the point late in the spring semester that my colleagues at Palestine High School warned me about. Their interest is low, their attention spans short, and their attitudes poor. We're finishing up our third week with Hamlet, and I guess my English IV kids' poor efforts represent one of the "slings and arrows of outrageous fortune" that he says we have to put up with.

"Harold is coming over," I say. "I promised him your barbecued chicken."

He smiles. "Then I guess I'd better get the fire started." He has, over long years of practice, perfected the cooking of chickens on an outdoor grill. Harold, a fellow first-year teacher who moved here from Oklahoma, is one of the biggest fans of his culinary talents. But then, Harold is one of the biggest of any fans of any number of things, weighing closer to three hundred pounds than two and standing a looming six feet six inches. He is appreciative of any food put before him, but he is particularly impressed with my father's barbecued chicken.

By the time Harold arrives, the baked beans are simmering in the oven, the green salad is tossed in its bowl, and the chickens are slowly cooking over glowing coals on the grill. We are soon sitting in lawn chairs in the backyard of my rented house, three teachers—two at the very beginning of their careers, one near the completion of his—at the end of their week.

A year ago, I wouldn't have predicted that I would be in this job, in this town. I had intended to teach English on the college level. As a matter of fact, I had applied for, and been awarded, a graduate fellowship in the English department, where I would teach English 101 during the day and attend graduate classes at night. Then I would apply for a position as an instructor, and commute to a university that offered doctorates in English. After all of that, with my head full of literature and my wall full of diplomas, I would just stay on at Sam, since, to my way of thinking, there is no better place to teach and learn.

But on my father's advice, I took the courses necessary to become certified as a public school teacher; he figured I'd better have a backup plan. I lived with him while completing my student teaching last year at Palestine

High School, and drove the twenty miles to school every day. On the first day of the semester, I asked him if he had any advice. He sipped his coffee, and gave it without a second thought. "Make friends with the janitor and the principal's secretary," he said. "They get more things done than anybody."

It was a good semester. When one of the senior English teachers announced her retirement, the principal offered the position to me, and I took it without hesitation. I contacted the chairman of the English department, resigned my fellowship, and told him I was putting my graduate studies on hold for a year or two.

The dogwood tree in the backyard of my rented house is in full blossom and the air is sweet with honeysuckle. My father keeps a careful watch over the chickens, prodding them gently now and then with a fork, and painting them often with the sauce that he made of vinegar, bits of chopped onion, Worcestershire sauce, lemon juice, ketchup, a little sugar, and a healthy splash of his beer. Harold and I have tried our hands at this on occasion, but have always come up short of the offering that he produces so effortlessly. On one such attempt, our final product was so bloody in the middle and charred on the outside that we threw the whole mess away and went for burgers at Dairy Queen.

He tends to his chicken and listens as we gripe about our students' dwindling performance. Harold tells of experiences much like the ones I've been having. "I'll swear," he finishes, "I don't think they even care that we're trying to teach them at all." I chime in with agreement.

"They don't," my father says, not taking his eyes off the chickens. We stare at him, hoping for something just a tad more positive from a teacher with so many years under his belt.

"They don't care at all," he adds, and looks at us. "Some of them might care later, when they've lived enough of life to look back on it, but some of them will never care." He slowly turns each piece of chicken, basting the sections with his sauce. "If you fellows are going to worry about who cares about what you're doing, then you've gotten yourselves into the wrong profession." He is through turning and basting, and he lowers the cover of the grill so the meat can bathe in the smoke. "Your job is to teach; that's what you signed a contract for, to do the best job that you can to get your subject into the kids. You have to care about them, but you can't be their buddy, or their father; they've already got buddies and fathers." We just stare at him. "Don't worry if they don't appreciate you, just worry if they don't learn."

I think of Oakwood, and of the many years that he taught there, and of the countless lives that he touched. "But you're appreciated by a whole town," I say. "How can you say that's not important?"

He purses his lips into his common attitude of concentration.

"I didn't say it's not important. It is, and I'm proud of it." He wipes his hands with a towel. "But that can't be your goal; you can't set out to be liked or respected. "You've got to always make it your first chore to be a good teacher." He folds the towel neatly and lays it on the tray beside the grill. "If you do that, and do a good job of it, then the appreciation will take care of itself."

After we've finished eating and Harold has gone to his garage apartment, my father and I stand by his car in the driveway. "Don't let the end of the year get you down," he tells me. "Being tired and aggravated in May is as natural as being eager to get at it in September. Everybody's worn down by now, the kids *and* the teachers."

He opens his car door, ready to drive the twenty miles to Oakwood.

"Teaching is a hard road," he says, leaning on the car door. "Whether it's teaching where you are now or at college. You'll never get rich at it, and it's rare that somebody will slap you on the back and say what a good job you're doing." He swats at a mosquito, and rubs the back of his neck with his hand. "And you have to be kind of special to be good at it." He lowers himself into the car; I put his small sack of groceries in the back seat. He rolls the window down and looks at me.

"I'll bet you're good at it," he says, before starting the car and driving away.

I bask in the glow of those six words for several minutes before I go into the house.

t w e l v e

November 1992   The phone call came at just after three in the morning on November tenth. I knew, of course, what it meant, knew so absolutely as I reached for the receiver that I would have been shocked if it had been anything else. The sound of the ring itself was shrill and quick, piercing sleep and night and security as only those types of calls do.

Janie's voice came tenuous and tired over the line. Alene had been called and told that he had "slipped away" just after the nurse had checked on him. I couldn't imagine him "slipping" anywhere, by accident, as if he simply forgot to draw his next breath. However he died, I imagined he had it planned and ordered so as not to cause anyone trouble.

Janie was not crying, and neither was I. But we were on that delicate verge of tears, both of us working hard to hold at bay the single gasp that would cause us to break down, as my father and I had, over the phone on that cold night when I had called him from Fort Dix. My sister and I said the words to each other that all families must say at one time or another. We agreed to talk later in the morning. Diane, she said, would call later.

After a few minutes with Karen, I went to the kitchen to make coffee. Wise Karen, who knew that this was time I had to spend alone. The cat, confused by this alteration in our daily routine, crept slowly behind, wondering what was up, and why *we* were up. She stretched and yawned all the way, making her point.

For years I had wondered what this moment would be like, this suddenly not having him in the world. Standing at the kitchen sink, I realized that it was not at all the way I had imagined. I knew a void, and a numbness, but no other feelings came. I tilted the three level measures of coffee into the clean filter and added the water, filled to the correct line on the glass pot. This was a ritual, as were the next things I did, filling the cat's food and water dishes, and winding the Navy clock. I hadn't asked anybody for the clock when we sold the Oakwood house after my father married Alene and moved to Longview. I figured that looking at it almost every day of my life gave me a right of ownership of sorts, so I unscrewed it from the wall and brought it home and put it up in my house. As I wound it that morning, one quick turn with its key, I thought of the thousands of mornings that he must have done the same thing, lifted the same key and made the same turn and, having finished, gently lowered the glass face and twisted its bolt shut.

I ran my hand slowly over the old clock and knew how

it was different, this feeling that I had wondered about and dreaded for so long.

I knew that it would no longer be "him." From now on, it would be things that reminded me of him, physical things like clocks and caps and frying pans, and the smell of food cooking on a grill, and cigar smoke. And it would be people, old men in airports or coffee shops who move at a slow gait as he did, and touch the wall to keep their balance. Grandfathers at school plays or ball games who stick their bottom lips out, just a bit, when they're proud or thoughtful. Any number of things and people would remind me of him, I knew. There would be ghosts everywhere.

When the coffee was done, and I held a steaming mug of it, I stood at the sink and looked into the foggy darkness of the morning through the window. I thought of how, so often, you hear of old people dying in the early morning, as if the coming dawn held some special promise for them. Or perhaps they wanted to complete just one last day before going, or wished to leave before facing the burden of another one.

As the cat purred and rubbed between my feet, I recalled a Sunday long ago, when I had been stationed in Germany in the Army. Several of us were having a few beers in a bar and were looking forward to the Super Bowl, which would be broadcast over Armed Forces Television later that evening. The game would be played at Rice Stadium in Houston, so I was particularly excited about it. As I walked toward the rest room in the back of the bar, I heard my mother call my name, distinctly, clearly. It was so real that I turned toward her, only to face a crowded, smoke-filled room. I mentioned it to one or two of my buddies, but the moment was quickly lost in the laughter and drinking. Hours later, several of us stopped at the kitchen door of the NCO club and bought fried egg sandwiches from the cook who always sold them to us, no doubt pocketing the money. We walked across the snow-covered street to our barracks holding the warm sandwiches wrapped in foil, like treasures. Our company commander, a captain, was sitting on my bunk waiting for me when we got there. He told me that my mother was dead. This was obviously one of the duties of a company commander, to go out on cold nights and tell boys about people dying back home. My captain wasn't very good at it, and I felt sorry for him. I tried to give him my sandwich, but he wouldn't take it. Of course, she would have died about the time that I heard her voice.

She had come to tell me goodbye, I guess. Or maybe to show me that everything was O.K. between us now. Maybe she came to forgive me.

Now, standing at the kitchen window, holding tight to the coffee mug, I listened hard for my father's voice, or for his presence. I had to smile when I felt and heard nothing. That, after all, wasn't his style. Through long years of order and preparation, he had made sure that all was as he wanted it, packed neatly away into proper places. I thought of him closing his desk drawer in the old Oakwood school and turning the small key. He knew that everything was where it should be; there was no need to reopen the drawer at the end of the day.

I looked at the time on the Navy clock. In another hour or so, Karen and the kids would have to get up and prepare for a normal Tuesday. My day would not be normal.

I poured a fresh cup of coffee and found the videotape of the old Oakwood home movies that Janie and Thomas had paid to have transferred from the big reels they were on to a cassette. I hadn't watched the tape in a long time, so I slipped it into the machine and sat in my favorite chair. The screen flickered and there we all were, in such a different time and place. Diane's kids and I were tearing into Christmas presents, flinging wrapping paper all over the place. Mother, in her orange housecoat, smiled and waved my father and his camera away. Janie hugged her knees and shivered in the cold morning. Diane and Jimmy sat close beside each other on the sofa. The fire which had been built with such precision blazed away, and the tree blinked and spoke through a hundred or so ornaments, of which perhaps five survived, in my sister's and my Christmas storage boxes in attics and closets.

After several minutes of those days had rolled across the screen, the image that I had been both hoping for and dreading appeared. Here, quite rare since he was almost always the photographer, was my father, frying sausages in his old iron skillet. He was at the stove, in the kitchen I remembered so clearly that I might well have been standing in it that morning. He was wearing a pair of khakis and a pullover pajama top.

I felt the cold dampness of tears on my face as I sat, mesmerized, and watched the tape. And the man frying the sausages looked at the camera and seemed to say, with those knowing eyes, that all was well and as it should be.

His funeral was simple, well ordered, and to the point, as his life had been. It was held in the small funeral home chapel at Alto, the little East Texas town where he had grown up in the first years of the century. The preacher was Tom Hill, the young fellow who had been a student preacher in Oakwood and had dragged me off to college with him. He wasn't particularly young anymore, but he was still a Methodist preacher, an associate in one of the most affluent congregations in Houston. He had simply said "yes" when I had called. Tom had buried my mother and married Karen and me. I figured this would complete his clerical duties to the family, at least for a while. There were many flowers; the card on one of the largest arrangements read "Oakwood Schools," and was all blue and gold, the school colors.

Many of the old-timers from Oakwood came either to the service or to sit with us in the funeral home parlor the night before. Everybody seemed to have a favorite story to tell about him, and he was the quiet hero of each one.

After the funeral we followed behind the hearse along

the winding country road out to the Shiloah Cemetery and gathered around the casket while Tom said a few last words. Then we said a final prayer, to send him on his way.

When just a few of us were left, I stood at the casket and looked beside it at my mother's grave. It would be easier to come here now, with both of them here. Something was better, something deep and meaningful, and impossible to explain. My grandparents' graves were a few feet away; their oldest son, my father's big brother, lay beside them. He had died not long after the First World War as a result of his exposure to mustard gas. Uncle Gaston and my other uncles and aunts were buried elsewhere. There must have been some Oakwood people who had wondered, when Mother was buried, why my father had chosen to have their grave sites in Alto after spending almost all of his life in another town. Those who knew him well hadn't had to wonder. The proximity of his mother's grave told that tale.

A slow breeze moved through the tall pines in the old cemetery. The whole place seemed anxious for us to go on about our business and leave these people to theirs. It is peaceful there, and quiet. If ghosts ever do come out, and talk to one another, and remember their lives, like something out of *Our Town*, the people buried here have a nice place to do it.

I ran my hand along the smooth casket and knew that he was fine wherever he was. I hoped that it was a place of order and goodness.

On the way home, driving through Oakwood, Karen and I noticed that a couple of the flags were at half-staff. He would have liked that. His life had been all bound up in flags. He had always flown his American flag over the porch at the Oakwood house on national holidays, and he had made it his personal business to raise and lower the flag at the school when he had been superintendent. As he got older, he flew the flag every day at his and Alene's house in Longview. Once, as we sat on the patio there, he had stared for a long time at the Stars and Stripes curling gracefully in the breeze. "That's the prettiest sight in the world," he said.

The owner of the funeral home had told me that since my father was a veteran a folded flag would be placed by his head in the casket. He asked me who I would like it to be presented to before burial. Remembering the long succession of flags that he had flown proudly, I told him to leave it where it was.

Driving through Oakwood, I recognized little of the town that I had known. Most of the stores from my childhood were closed, and a few new ones occupied the old buildings. A modern gas station and mini-mart seemed to be the center of activity. The Methodist church, too big for its small congregation, stood lonely on its corner. It no longer had a full-time pastor; a lay preacher from another town came each Sunday morning to preside over the dozen or so old folks who sat in a small cluster in the front rows of the huge sanctuary. Miss Mae went every week, though she told me she couldn't quite see the preacher or hear what he was saying. She had called the funeral home on the night before the service and talked to Diane and Janie and me. Her failing health prevented her from coming to Alto; she cried when she talked to us, and I imagined her sitting in her favorite overstuffed chair in the den of her big house, clutching the reading glasses that were of little use to her now.

The white frame house that I grew up in beside Highway 79 caught the late afternoon sun. A lazy cat, coiled into a comfortable position, dozed under the porch swing where Bo used to take his naps. A pickup truck sat where the school car used to be.

Driving up the hill toward Buffalo, I thought of the town that I was leaving behind, and the man. Some of Oakwood's people would think of him tonight as they ate their suppers and sat before their television sets, but many of the current residents hadn't known him. The students that he had taught had left the school and the town to other generations who would not recognize his name. But the good that he had done there, in his quiet and orderly manner, would touch them. The values that he had helped to instill would, in some indirect way, be their values. That is the blessing of a life well lived; it is still here, even when the person is not.

Late that night, when Karen and the girls were sound asleep, I wound the Navy clock in our kitchen and fed the cat. In the morning, I would return to my classes, and to the fellowship of the teachers' workroom, and to the normality of my life. The bells would ring, and students would move through the hallways to their classes, and the daily business of education would go on. Eventually, they would leave for college or jobs, and then the years would pass and they would raise families and, with each passing year, would forget the people who taught them, except for a special one or two who put more into them than the material covered in textbooks.

Looking out the kitchen window into the dark ending of the long day, the Navy clock ticking as quietly as a heart beside me, I knew that when I stood before my classes in the morning, and all the mornings that would come after it, I would not be alone.

t h i r t e e n

I am searching in the clear summer sky for the small plane. Only a few cars are parked in front of the little county airport, so I know that he will probably be the sole passenger. I've made this hop to the big airport in Houston several times, and the pilots and I usually have the plane to ourselves. Finally, a tiny dot appears in the north, gradually becoming bigger and then becoming a two-engine plane. It lands on the narrow runway, taxis to the end of it, and makes a bumpy, wide turn before pulling up to the small terminal.

The pilot steps out first, then helps my father down from the doorway. He hesitates a moment, to get his bearings after the cramped flight, then walks toward the building. The older he gets—he's almost eighty now— the more he resembles George Burns when he walks. His legs shuffle along at their own slow pace, while his arms and upper torso appear to be anxious to get on with it. He is dressed in light summer slacks and a short-sleeved knit shirt. He smiles when he sees me, and waves.

"How was your flight?" I ask him, shaking his hand.

"Real good," he says, looking back at the plane. "The first one was a lot bigger than this one." He has flown two commuter flights, one from Longview to Houston, and then from Houston to Lake Jackson. He has never flown before today.

In the car, on the way to my place, he studies the landscape. "This is mighty fine country," he says.

"Flat and hot," I tell him. "I hope you brought cool clothes." It is July, and we haven't had a good rain for weeks. Everything is parched on the Gulf coast.

"Alene made sure I did," he says.

"What did you think of flying?" I ask him.

He smiles. "It hurt my ears." He continues to look out the window of the car. "I got to see lots of country. There weren't any clouds."

I tell him that we've forgotten what clouds look like.

"We'll go to Galveston tomorrow and have some seafood."

"Good," he says, and continues to look at the scenery.

In my apartment, I watch him unpack his suitcase and arrange his clothes in neat stacks in the chest of drawers of the spare bedroom.

"Do you recognize the furniture?" I ask him.

He looks around the room at the cherry-wood pieces. He nods and smiles. This is the bedroom furniture from my old room in Oakwood. We kids divided up the loot when he sold the house and moved to Longview. He sees the new drafting table covered with papers and pens by the window.

"Do you do much drawing?" he asks. I tell him I teach a calligraphy class at the junior college and do illustration workshops for children at the local art league studio.

"Good," he says, picking up one of the parchments and studying it. "Your mother would have been happy about that." She had always wanted me to become a commercial artist and to write and illustrate children's books. He puts the paper exactly back where he got it.

"Now, don't you let me keep you from your usual routine," he says. "I'll be happy here just reading the newspaper and watching television."

"You are my routine for the next couple of days," I tell him. "I've been looking forward to this." It took considerable encouragement to get him to make this trip. I taught the first session of summer school and have several weeks off before the school year starts in August. After numerous phone calls, I finally persuaded him to fly down for a few days. It's been a while since just the two of us have spent any time together.

This is my fifth year as an English teacher and tennis coach at Brazoswood High School. It's been ten years since I made that promise to the chairman of the English department at Sam Houston. I didn't keep it. I never went back to graduate school, never became the professor that I had always intended to be.

Later, as I am putting together something for our dinner, he calls to me from the living room. "You sure have lots of movies." I know that he is looking at the long row of videotapes over the television.

"We'll watch one tonight if you want to," I call from the kitchen. I know that he isn't big on movies, and I thought we might watch the Astros game on television. I don't have anything taped with his old friend Dana Andrews in it; neither do I have any Francis (the Talking Mule) or Ma and Pa Kettle epics.

He comes into the kitchen with a tape. It is *On Golden Pond*, with Henry Fonda and Katharine Hepburn. "I always liked these two," he says.

After dinner, as I am putting the tape into the machine, he asks which chair is mine. He has a special chair in his house, as he always did in Oakwood, and everyone, by unspoken agreement, stays out of it.

"I don't have a favorite," I tell him. "Take any one you want." He waits until I sit down, just in case I'm not telling him the truth. Then he makes himself comfortable on the couch.

He seems to enjoy the movie. I notice that he pays close attention during the part where Henry Fonda's character becomes lost on a familiar trail, wanders frantically through the woods, and ends up at his cabin, telling his wife that he had been afraid.

At the end of it, while I am rewinding the tape, he looks at his watch and says it's past his bedtime. I tell him to make himself at home; I've put today's *Houston Post* on the bedside table.

After my shower, I stop by his room to say good night. He is propped up on the pillows; the newspaper is in his hands, but he doesn't seem to be reading it. His wallet is on top of the chest of drawers, his handkerchief folded neatly beside it. Several coins, stacked perfectly, are on the handkerchief, alongside his pocket comb and penknife. It all looks like instruments that have been laid out for a particularly fussy surgeon.

"About to call it a night?" I ask him.

He folds the paper, and takes off his glasses. "I was just thinking about that movie," he says, rubbing his eyes.

"It's a good one," I say.

"I don't think they should have had that boy use that sort of language," he says. The young actor in the film uses some words that he is not used to hearing, especially from children.

"Lots of kids talk that way," I tell him, thinking of some of the conversations I hear in the halls at school.

He seems to be thinking this over. "I hope I never get like that," he says. This confuses me; if he has lived nearly eighty years without relying on vulgarity to communicate, surely he can make it the rest of the way. Then I realize that he's not talking about the boy.

"Do you mean the man Henry Fonda played?" I ask him.

He nods yes. "Old people get like that sometimes."

"Well," I say, "I can't imagine you getting like that. You have a better memory than I do."

"You can't ever tell," he says, turning off the lamp beside his bed. "I'll put up a fight against it if it starts to happen."

In my own bed, I wonder if he has started to forget

things. This certainly doesn't seem to be so; he appears to be as in control as he's always been. Two or three days after Mother's funeral, he went to town to buy some groceries, paid for them, and came home without them. It embarrassed him, and it bothered him for several days. He was, of course, just preoccupied about her death; we all were. But he may have seen it as an omen of the worst possibility that he could imagine: the loss of independence and dignity.

I've often wondered if part of his fear of getting sick has to do with the fact that it might mean having to delegate responsibility for himself to other people, like doctors and nurses and family. He's never been good at delegation. I told him once about the principal at the school where I was working taking a vote of the faculty to get their opinion on something he was thinking about implementing. "Why?" my father asked, in all sincerity. The new concept of site-based management would not have made sense to him. To his way of thinking, teachers are paid to teach, and administrators are paid to run the school. He reads no more pomp or dignity into one than the other, and sees both as high callings.

I turn off the lamp and listen for the snoring from down the hall that is one of the hymns of my life, but there is only silence.

In the morning, we drive to Galveston along a stretch of road known as the Blue Water Highway. Seagulls sail along over the surface of the water, dipping in every so often for an inattentive mullet. Several shrimp boats sit on the horizon.

He takes it all in as we move between the Gulf of Mexico and all the hotels and motels and shops of Seawall Boulevard. We came here when I was growing up, three days each summer, and stayed in either the Galvez or the Buccaneer. He and Janie and I would spend hours in the surf while Mother, not a swimmer, would amble along the beach in one of her orange sundresses, picking up shells.

After riding the ferry to Point Bolivar and back—a favorite expedition of my father's in Galveston—we go for lunch to one of the trendy seafood places overlooking the Gulf. He is unhappy about the quantity of food we receive on our Fisherman Platters. In his opinion, a person should get what a person pays for. The prices are high here, and he feels the two small shrimp, a sliver of fish, and a tiny stuffed crab straight from the freezer are not worth the amount being charged.

"It sure didn't used to be this way," he says, thinking of our old Galveston trips.

"Unfortunately," I say, still hungry as I push the empty plate away, "that's the way it is these days."

"It shouldn't be," is all he has to say about it.

Later, we walk along the seawall and watch the waves roll up on the island. The beach is full of people, and the breeze off the Gulf is stiff. He looks at all of it for a long time, and I know that he must be thinking about our trips down here. I wonder if he can almost see, as I can right now, Mother ambling along the shore, her bright orange scarf billowing out behind her like a sail.

We are standing in the small terminal of the county airport, waiting for the call for his flight. There are a few more people milling around than usual, so he'll have some company this time.

"I brought the morning paper," I tell him. "In case you want to read it on the plane."

"I don't need it," he says. "I'll be looking out the window."

"Do you have everything?" I ask him.

"Yep," he says, patting the small suitcase. I know that everything is folded neatly inside, along with the box of chocolate-covered cashews he bought for Alene at the mall last night. He told the young salesgirl he wanted "ca*shoos*"; I believe she thought he was sneezing.

"I've really enjoyed your visit," I say.

"I did, too." He checks his ticket for the fifth or sixth time. We look out the window at the small plane, knowing that it will only be a moment before they call him.

"Sometimes I wish you didn't live so far away," he tells me. This is as close as he can come to saying he misses me.

"It's not that far," I say. "I'll just have to do better about getting up there for visits."

He nods that this is a good idea.

"There's one thing I wanted to ask you," he says after a moment. The pilot opens the doors of the terminal, and several people move in their direction. He watches them for a moment, so I have to wait for his question. Finally, he turns his attention back to me, and asks it. "Are you happy at teaching?" He picks up his suitcase. "Are you glad you did it?"

"Very happy," I tell him. "Very glad."

He smiles. "That's good," he says. "I always liked it." He's retired now. He watches the passengers getting into the plane. He looks at his ticket one last time and turns it in his hand. "I sure miss it."

He looks up from his ticket and gives a brief nod. I wonder if it means "Have to be going now." I wonder if it means "Nothing lasts forever."

"I know," I say.

We shake hands and he walks, like George Burns, out to the plane. I watch as the pilot helps him into the door.

Outside, I stand by the car and watch the little plane take off. I watch it until it is nothing more than a dot in the hot July afternoon sky. And then it is gone.

Acknowledgments

Special thanks to Jason Rekulak, who patiently waded through the first draft with me; to Jon Hodges, who prodded my memory by mapping out, on butcher paper, the Oakwood of our youth; to Ethan Nosowsky, my editor at Farrar, Straus and Giroux, for taking the chance on a long shot; and, always, to Karen, for reading every page as it came.

lle, Ron,
2 -

that good
ht.

$22.00

DATE			